MW01029730

ADOBE!

*Homes and Interiors
of Taos, Santa Fe and
the Southwest*

The formal entry of the Seth home in Santa Fe sits on a level above the large living room. An antique Mexican bench is covered with a Saltillo blanket of eye-dazzler pattern.

ADOBE!

HOMES AND INTERIORS OF TAOS, SANTA FE AND ◥◤ THE SOUTHWEST ◢◣

By SANDRA and LAUREL SETH

Illustrations by Valerie Graves

ARCHITECTURAL BOOK PUBLISHING COMPANY
Stamford, Connecticut 06903

Acknowledgments

We would like to thank our parents, Oliver and Jean Seth, for their support and encouragement; Valerie Graves for her invaluable artistic and photographic contributions; and Kristina Wilson for all of her help.

We are grateful to the many people who, over the last four years, generously allowed us to photograph their homes, and to the museums and foundations which also permitted us to include them. We owe a great deal of thanks to the three artists who shared part of their lives with us—Virginia Romero, Teresa Archuleta-Sagel and Georgia O'Keeffe. Also, Mariano Mirabel, Mrs. Pablo Quintana and Louis Cottam gave us more than could ever appear in their portraits.

Dan Budnick gave us a wonderful photograph of Miss O'Keeffe, and Mid Reitz donated a beautiful color transparency of a Mexican doorway.

There are many others who helped us along the way. We would like to thank each one sincerely. A partial list is offered here: Edwin Bewley; Jean Burgess; the Hahns; Juan Hamilton; Sally Hyer; Kit Carson Foundation—Neil Pose; Lightworks; the Lyons; Robin Martin; Steve McDowell; Melody at Webb Design; Museum of New Mexico Archives—Richard Rudisell and Art Olivas; School of American Research, Santa Fe; Ed Smith; Ros Spicer; Rita Sutcliff and Louise Trigg.

Our publisher, Walter Frese, has been thoughtful and accessible throughout the process.

Thank you, Meliton Montano, even though you can't read this.

Copyright © 1988 by Sandra and Laurel Seth, All rights reserved. No part of this publication may be reproduced, stored in a retrieval system, or transmitted, in any form or by any means, electronic, mechanical, photocopying, recording or otherwise, without the prior permission of the copyright owners or the publishers.

Architectural Book Publishing Company, Inc.
268 Dogwood Lane, Stamford, CT., 06903.

Printed in the United States of America

10   9   8   7   6   5

Library of Congress Cataloging-in-Publication Data

Seth, Sandra, 1948–
  Adobe! Homes and Interiors of Taos, Santa Fe, and the Southwest by Sandra and Laurel Seth; with illustrations by Valerie Graves.
    p.   cm.
  Bibliography: p.
  Includes index.
  ISBN 0-942655-00-1
  1. Adobe houses—New Mexico. 2. Architecture, Domestic—New Mexico. 3. Vernacular architecture—New Mexico. 4. Interior decoration—New Mexico. 5. Adobe houses—Southwest, New. 6. Architecture, Domestic—Southwest, New. 7. Vernacular architecture—Southwest, New. 8. Interior decoration—Southwest, New. I. Seth, Laurel, 1953–   . II. Title.
NA7235.N6S48 1988
728.3' 7' 09789 – dc19   87-37421   CIP

Contents

Foreword

The old-timers—Indian, Hispanic and Anglo—showed me how to build with adobe, how to make fireplaces, and how to plaster with mud. The years spent building without a crew—some 6 houses and 150 fireplaces—just increased my love for adobe: for the flexible, sculptural potential of mud; the comforting and invigorating feeling of living surrounded by earth; and the connection to the other cultures and peoples which both the style and the material give us.

They say it gets in your blood, and you keep adding onto your house, and when that's too big, you build another adobe house somewhere. The feel of mud and the results of building with it are psychologically and physically rewarding, so much so that this book directly sprang from that addiction to and affection for adobe, the material.

The effect of living in an adobe, which is traditional and has traditional elements within it, and the connection with diverse cultures, the ties with more than just the present are realizations that came to me subtly but surely.

When architecture or architectural elements have such rich associations and impart so much to those living within and around them, it is horrible to see them die or change almost beyond recognition. These elements with old and distinct qualities are the architectural "traditions" we explore in this book. We hope by doing so to encourage their continued creation.

Sandy Seth
Taos, New Mexico

The American Southwest is culturally unique, and architecture is an insepa-
rable and lasting expression of its tricultural heritage.

Our family has been in New Mexico for three generations, a short time in
comparison with Mrs. Pablo Quintana's and Teresa Archuleta-Sagel's Hispanic
roots, and shorter yet than Virginia Romero and Mariano Mirabal's Indian heritage, yet we feel somehow deeply connected to each of these cultures. It is as
much because of what we live in and see around us—architecture from a long
tradition that does not dominate the landscape, but is *of* the landscape—as it
is knowing individuals within all three cultures.

Our motivation in writing this book was twofold; we wanted to explore and
share our love for traditional adobe architecture, and also give credit to each
culture's architectural contributions by focusing on representative individuals
within each culture. In a special chapter, we feature three artists from the three
core cultures of the Southwest, working in three different artistic expressions—
a potter, a weaver and a painter who are an Indian, an Hispanic and an Anglo:
Virginia Romero, Teresa Archuleta-Sagel and Georgia O'Keeffe. All have responded strongly to the earth, and have made it part of their lives, homes and
works. So our book is about more than architecture, it is also about the reason
for architecture—people.

We hope to reveal very personal elements innate in earth architecture,
and to emphasize the specialness of building with adobe. The traditional styles
and adaptations of these styles which we explore in this book are those that
maintain a distinct connection with the past, elements with old and distinct
characteristics.

Many varieties of each component of an adobe house are shown in historical
progression. We felt this order gives clearer credit to the tricultural origins of
our present-day architecture. We have also tried to simplify the use of this
book as a reference tool by placing each ingredient in an adobe home in a
separate chapter.

We hope, for more than just aesthetic reasons, that our Southwest, now
confronted by so much potentially alienating architectural change, will maintain and
repeat the beautiful and satisfying heritage of its past.

Laurie and Sandy Seth

Introduction

"We have lived upon this land from days beyond history's records, far past any living memory, deep into the time of legend. The story of my people and the story of this place are one single story. No man can think of us without thinking of this place. We are always joined together." This is the statement of a Taos Pueblo man.

So it is in much of southwestern North America. Here Indian people remain in their traditional homelands, and much that is vital in life remains as it was, timeless. Here is the oldest continuous record of human habitation, which has fashioned this region into a humanized landscape suffused with ancient meanings, myths and mysteries.

When the Southwest was first seen with European eyes, those of Francisco Vasques de Coronado and the men of his expedition of 1540, both the land and the people of the Southwest were already very diverse and very old. One has only to think of the great multihued gaps in the earth, such as Bryce and the Grand Canyon, Zion and Canyon de Chelly, or of the gigantic and majestic spires of red sandstone comprising nature's own sculpture in Monument Valley, to slip into a geological time perspective. One's spatial sense as well as one's temporal sense grows immense in the Southwest before the vast distances and topographical diversity that open out before one's eyes when looking down from any high vantage point. Here, truly, the imagination soars and the very spirit is set free. The spirit is further moved, and the temporal sense is further broadened, by contemplation of the various native groups upon this land, many of whom were encountered in 1540 near where they are, and living very much as they do in the last quarter of the twentieth century.

The Pueblo peoples are the only one of the cultural groups, identifiable as long ago as two millennia, that have survived with clearly unbroken cultural continuity into the last quarter of the twentieth century. In their greatest time, from the tenth through the thirteenth centuries, they built and occupied the great architectural wonders at Chaco Canyon, Mesa Verde, Casa Grande, and numerous other places spread out over what are now five large states. During this time they ranged from mountain to canyon and even to the higher desert elevations. During the persistent drought that haunted the Southwest in the last quarter of the thirteenth century, the Pueblo people began contracting into the great valley of the Rio Grande and its tributaries. Only the Hopi, then as now, enigmatically hung on and persisted in farming successfully in a region with no permanent or semipermanent watercourses.

The other Pueblo groups maintained their way of life—characterized in essence by intensive horticulture, an elaborate ceremonial cycle, and a cohesive social organization—in the villages of adobe and stone that, for the most part, are strung along the Rio Grande and its tributaries like beads on a crooked string.

The special relationship with the land that the people of San Juan and, indeed, of all the Pueblos, have is reflected in the way in which the villages, as architectural entities, are distributed upon the land. These villages of adobe blend so well with their surroundings that it is impossible to spot them on the ground from more than a few hundred feet away. This is so despite the fact that they are all built on level ground elevated slightly from the nearby watercourses, and it is as true for Taos, with its twin five-story apartment buildings, and for the large Keresan Pueblos, as it is for the smaller and more dispersed Tewa Pueblos. Obviously, this camouflaging, brought about as much through the use of natural building materials as it was through careful site selection, was necessary when the Pueblos were engaged in intermittent defensive warfare with the Navajo, Apache and some Southern Plains nations. But still in the 1980s this building pattern conveys a sense of being a part of the earth itself and, therefore, of fading into the landscape. The only buildings that do not fit this pattern are some churches and structures erected of nontraditional materials in nontraditional ways since the midnineteenth century.

The architecture of the Pueblos is gentle and unobtrusive as are the Pueblo peoples' very character, customs, institutions and art forms. The Pueblo peoples have shown a genius for maintaining that which is most essential to their lives while also receiving, absorbing, and reinvigorating the decaying "vines"—to use the appropriate and evocative Tewa metaphor—of other ways of life. Hence, the Pueblo legacy has been to endure.

Dr. Alfonso Ortiz is Professor of Anthropology at the University of New Mexico. Dr. Ortiz is a Pueblo Indian from the Tewa village of San Juan, north of Santa Fe, New Mexico.

Adobe in the Southwest

Adobe architecture houses almost half of the world's population today. Adobe is a reshaped and hardened material made of the earth itself; adobe buildings grow out of the very landscape on which they rest, their flexible and sensual shapes blending with their surroundings. There are examples of earth architecture on every continent, each expressing the culture, people and environment of its area.

Southwestern architecture is a blend of sensibilities and technologies from three cultures: Native American, Spanish and Anglo. Even the word "adobe" is a cultural hybrid, believed to come from the Egyptian hieroglyph denoting brick, which, translated into Arabic, becomes *at-tob* or *al-tob* meaning sun-dried brick. The Moors then brought the word and the technique to Spain where it became *adobar*, meaning to daub, plaster or knead. Today, the word "adobe" is used to describe the mud, the brick, and the buildings made from them.

Builders in the Southwest have utilized the earth at hand for thousands of years in many forms: pit houses, cave dwellings, earthen pueblos, mud-covered hogans, adobe haciendas, stores and mansions. Remarkably, the tradition of building with adobe continues to evolve in this area. It is the medium of adobe that is the common factor. Mud is a practical medium, a flexible medium and, most importantly, an organic medium. Anyone who has known an earth dwelling remembers its coolness in summer and warmth in winter, and its solace for the soul. These feelings, so difficult to describe, are the heart of the experience of adobe. Some of the feeling comes from the softness of line in the walls, lines that echo those in nature and so are soothing and familiar. Some of the feeling comes from the harmonious colors, which originate in the landscape. The sense of touch is richly rewarded, for adobe is a tactile and sculptural presence. Adobe ties earth to earth, producing a form that shelters and comforts humans in many parts of the globe.

Indians in the Southwest

Already 25,000 years ago there were in the Southwest hunters and gatherers, following herds of game, harvesting wild crops and seeking shelter in caves. It is unknown when the first man-made buildings were constructed, but the earliest structural remains that have been found are of pit houses 10,000 years old. An increasing reliance on domesticated crops of maize and squash, introduced from Mexico, resulted in population increases, and the need for more permanent settlements. When crop irrigation became a factor, river drainages became preferred building sites. Snaketown, a Hohokam village on the Salt River in Arizona, was occupied year-round by 300 B.C., but most southwestern sites remained seasonal for another thousand years, until agriculture became more reliable and trade networks were established.

When centralized towns and trading centers were built, they were spectacular. Cliff Palace, at Mesa Verde in Colorado, constructed of stone, mortared and plastered with mud, contained 200 rooms and stood three stories high. The perfectly preserved fingerprints of its eleventh-century builders are still visible in the adobe. Another advance trading center was located in Chaco Canyon, New Mexico. A network of ancient "roads" converges there, and the influence of its masonry and architectural style is evident in sites hundreds of miles apart. The stonework at Chaco and its many pueblo outliers is complex and beautiful; selected stones were laid in mud mortar, often in patterns. Surprisingly, these elaborate surfaces were then plastered with mud. One of the key elements of Chaco architecture is its great kivas, huge subterranean ceremonial rooms that measure up to 63 feet in diameter. Great kivas, which originated at Chaco Canyon, are found from Colorado to Southern Arizona.

The role of warfare in the Southwest during the 1200s and 1300s has not been fully explored, but it is known that many early sites were defensible; they were located on steep cliff faces and mesa tops, or had a network of sentry outposts. Multistoried pueblos had rooftop entrances that were easily defensible when ladders were withdrawn, while windows were small or nonexistent.

Whether as a result of warfare, a sudden change in climate, or some still unexplained mystery, the cities of this era were abandoned. It is thought that the people who left moved south and established the present-day pueblos along the Rio Grande and on the Hopi mesas. What is known is that by 1275 the pueblos of Taos and Pecos were under construction. When the Spanish arrived in 1540, they found over 125 occupied pueblos in the region, most built of adobe, some up to seven stories high.

The Apaches and Navajos arrived only shortly before the Spanish expeditions, and maintained their nomadic way of life throughout the period of Spanish settlement. They built temporary ramadas of cedar and thatchwork and, occasionally, more permanent dwellings of mud and brush, called hogans. Many Navajos today still live in hogans scattered throughout their almost four-million-acre reservation.

All native American dwellings utilized the earth; the soil became the walls or plaster, the cave wall or quarried stone became the walls or floor, and the timber became the walls or roof. As a result, these homes and villages seem to emerge from the landscape.

Mariano Mirabal of Taos Pueblo replastering the *horno* (outdoor adobe oven) he and his wife, Rufina, built in 1970. As well as playing an important role in Taos Pueblo ceremonial activities, Mr. Mirabal still plows his fields with a team of horses and shares his wealth of traditional building knowledge with others.

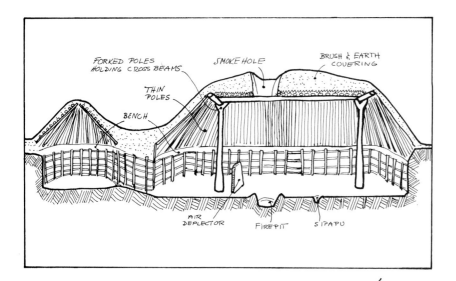

FORKED POLES
HOLDING CROSS BEAMS

SMOKEHOLE

BRUSH & EARTH
COVERING

THIN
POLES

BENCH

AIR
DEFLECTOR

FIREPIT

SIPAPU

This drawing represents a hypothetical floor plan of a prehistoric pit house, circa 450 A.D. Pit houses are the earliest architectural remains found in the Southwest. *Adapted from an illustration in "Early Architecture in New Mexico" by Bainbridge Bunting, courtesy University of New Mexico Press.*

Taos Pueblo, *right*, constructed of puddled adobe, has been occupied since at least 1300. Coronado stayed here during his expedition of 1540. Fray Dominguez reported in 1776 that North and South Pueblos were connected by a wall, with towers where the wall met the Rio Pueblo.

North Pueblo, *right*, stands about five stories high and eleven rooms wide. South Pueblo is four stories high and roughly triangular in shape. The Rio Pueblo, which flows from sacred Blue Lake, runs through the center of the pueblo. *Photos, courtesy Museum of New Mexico, neg number 16707, neg number 91966.*

Betatakin Ruin is one of the largest prehistoric cliff dwellings in existence. Its 150 rooms are built in a cave 450 feet long and 150 feet deep. Tree ring dates of Betatakin place its occupation from about 1260 to 1277. Now a part of Navajo National Monument, it was probably inhabited by the ancestors of today's Pueblo Indians.

A kiva at San Ildefonso Pueblo, New Mexico. Kivas are ceremonial chambers, usually round and partially subterranean. They are entered by ladder from the roof. This kiva was described by Castano de Sosa, Spanish explorer, on his 1540 expedition. *Photo by T. Harmon Parkhurst, courtesy Museum of New Mexico, neg number 3693.*

The San Estevan del Rey Mission Church in Acoma, New Mexico. The mission was constructed under the direction of Fray Juan Ramirez between 1629 and 1642. This is one of the best preserved and least altered missions in the Southwest and served as the model for Pueblo Revival-style architecture. The walls of the mission stand 35 feet high and the interior worshiping space is 150 by 40 feet. All construction materials were transported to the sheer-cliffed mesa top by Indian laborers. *Photo by Wyatt Davis, ca. 1945, courtesy Museum of New Mexico, neg number 3046.*

Mrs. Pablo Quintana, 92, sits on the second-story balcony of her Territorial adobe in El Salto, New Mexico. The house was begun when she was six years old. She helped to mix the mud for the adobes, using the earth where the house now stands, land that has been in her family for hundreds of years.

Hispanics in the Southwest

The Spanish explorers, known as conquistadores, entered what is now New Mexico in 1540. In 1598, a band of colonists led by Don Juan de Oñate came to stay, bringing with them livestock, firearms, and a complex blend of European and Moorish cultural elements.

Their first colony was established in part of the Pueblo Indian town of Yungue-Ouinge, near the confluence of the Rio Grande and Chama Rivers. Eleven years later, in 1610, construction was begun on the permanent settlement at Santa Fe, and the Palace of the Governors (still in use today) dates from that year.

Early Hispanic building was strongly influenced by defensive necessities; thick walls, small doorways and sparing use of windows were standard. This same consideration led to the creation of a new style of religious architecture —the fortress church, intended to shelter a town's citizens and its livestock when necessary. Franciscan friars became some of the Southwest's most ambitious builders, beginning the construction of mission churches in the Indian pueblos almost immediately after their arrival in the 1580s. These impressive structures are a hybrid of medieval fortification and the styles of the Pueblo builders.

Spanish introductions in the early period include wooden forms used to cast adobe as bricks (in contrast to the Pueblos' puddling technique), chimneyed fireplaces, *hornos* for outside baking, and an array of metal tools. Their horses, cattle, sheep and goats altered both the architectural necessities and the landscape.

The scale of Spanish construction ranged from small single-family ranchos to large haciendas built around a central *placita,* often incorporating a defensive *torreón* (tower) as a feature. The Martinez Hacienda at Taos and the Rancho de las Golondrinas near Santa Fe are good examples. A collection of single-family dwellings was often grouped around a central plaza as well, with the structures joined by common walls. The Plaza de Cerro in Chimayo and the Plaza at Costilla, New Mexico, are typical of this arrangement.

The harsh environment of the Southwest requires frugality, and efficient architecture. The Hispanic people responded to this by taking advantage of south-facing building sites, and establishing communities near, but not on, scarce arable land. The remoteness of the frontier colony resulted in an architectural conservatism that lasted for over 200 years, until new immigrants arrived from the East bringing a vast array of new materials and building styles. Even then, traditional forms were not rejected, and wonderful hybrids like the Victorian-style adobes in mountain villages of New Mexico appeared. Today, the tradition of the early colonists is reaffirmed through a renaissance of architectural and artistic expression.

San Francisco de Assisi Mission Church in Ranchos de Taos, New Mexico. Built in 1772, this sculptural church back has been a popular subject for paintings and photographs throughout the years. Because of a near devastating experience with cement plaster, the church is annually replastered with mud by the community.

San Xavier del Bac Mission in Arizona, constructed between 1700 and 1797 in a cruciform shape. The design is a distinctive Mexican baroque combination of Moorish, Italian, Flemish and Spanish elements. Built of fired adobe bricks and plastered with white lime, the surfaces are adorned with elaborate plaster relief carvings, pilasters and panels. Interior walls were polished with river stones and painted with earth pigments.

Carmel Mission in California. The mission of San Carlos Borromeo, established by Fray Junípero Serra, was the headquarters of the padre and, as such, was the most important of the California missions. The buildings were constructed between 1793 and 1797 of fired adobe bricks in a typical northern Mexican style. *Photo by Lewis Josselyn, courtesy Museum of New Mexico, neg number 14980.*

The *torreón* (defensive tower) at Rancho de las Golondrinas. Built from the red clay layers of La Cienega, New Mexico, this seventeenth-century house surrounds a protective *placita* area. Small windows for observation face the fields below.

Part of Rancho de las Golondrinas, a large complex of traditional adobe buildings owned and managed by the Old Cienega Village Museum. Golondrinas was a *paraje* (stopping place) on the Camino Real from Mexico originally obtained through royal purchase in 1710 by the Vega y Coca family.

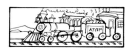

Anglos in the Southwest

Even before the United States Constitution was written, restless American trappers and traders were attracted to the Southwest. For over 100 years, the merchants of Chihuahua enjoyed a monopoly, enforced by the Spanish crown, on the trading market, but by the 1820s wagon trains loaded with goods from St. Louis and the East Coast began arriving on the Santa Fe plaza to conduct unsanctioned trade. The response to cheaper staples and new merchandise was so great that fences were erected around the plaza to protect what little grass was left from mule and oxen traffic. In 1821, the Mexican Government officially recognized the Santa Fe Trail, and a steady stream of new materials became available throughout the Southwest. New Mexican architecture was quick to reflect the impact of the Santa Fe Trail trade. Window glass was in use in the customs house on the Santa Fe plaza as early as 1837, and by 1846 most of the mica windows in the Palace of the Governors were replaced with glass.

A new vocabulary of architectural styles emerged, partly a result of the construction of large military complexes by the United States Government after the Mexican War ended in 1848, when Mexico ceded the area that is now New Mexico, Utah, Nevada, Arizona and California to the United States. These territorial forts, which included their own lumber and brick mills, were built in a modification of the Greek Revival style popular on the East Coast. Its architectural hallmarks included brick coping, double-hung windows and wood floors, but the most distinctive feature of this new "Territorial Style" was the decorative wood trim which adorned both exterior and interior surfaces, and which quickly developed into a showcase for folk motifs.

The railroad brought swift changes wherever its tracks were laid, and the Southwest was no exception. Established farming and ranching communities like Albuquerque and Las Vegas, New Mexico, changed dramatically when the railroad arrived in 1880. New and remodeled houses soon sported many new features: ready-made doors and windows, cheap glass, lathe and band-saw fashioned wood, cast-iron columns, pressed metal ceilings, corrugated iron roofs, hardwood floors, cement foundations, oil paint, wallpaper, iron stoves, furnaces, gas fixtures and plumbing.

By 1900 the influence of the railroad was exemplified in a style of its own called "Mission Revival," begun in California in the 1890s and adopted by the Santa Fe Railroad as the signature style of its own station buildings. One of the finest examples was the Alvarado Hotel in Albuquerque, finished in 1902. Tragically, the building was razed in 1970 for a parking lot.

The turn of the century also saw professional architects utilizing elements of native styles. In 1905, on the south rim of the Grand Canyon, Mary Colter built "Hopi House," modeled after the mesa-top pueblos of the Hopi Indians. John Gaw Meem remodeled Hodgin Hall at the University of New Mexico in 1908 into one of the earliest examples of "Pueblo Revival" architecture. After New Mexico became the 47th state in 1912, the trend was solidified when Rapp and Rapp, architects, using the Acoma Mission church as their inspiration,

A load of delicious piñon nuts from Northern New Mexico sits loaded and ready for shipment in this 1913 photo. Mr. Gormley and a friend drive the mule wagon in front of the Palace of the Governors on the plaza in Santa Fe. The Palace was constructed in 1610. *Photo by Jesse L. Nusbaum, 1913, courtesy Museum of New Mexico, neg number 61440.*

Louie Cottam of Taos, New Mexico. In 1918 Mr. Cottam rode the Chili line, a narrow-gauge railroad, to Tres Piedras near Taos to join the Forest Service. Since that time he has designed and supervised the building of over 15 adobe homes in the Taos area, using local Indian and Hispanic builders, including Annie Archuleta, the well-respected builder of traditional adobe fireplaces.

presented the New Mexico building at the San Diego Exposition. It was the hit of the show with its sensual adobe lines and huge carved vigas. Colorful Indian dancers performed there each day, and the building was filled with popular displays of Indian arts and crafts. The same exposition building design was used in 1917 for the Fine Arts Museum on the Santa Fe plaza, which, though not adobe, epitomizes Pueblo Revival architecture.

By the 1930s many artists had settled in the Southwest, drawn by its unique culture and architecture. American expatriates returning from Europe and health-seekers from the cities of the Midwest and the East fostered a major crafts revival. Aided by government programs of the period, they documented traditional architecture and encouraged traditional expressions in furniture making, door making, weaving and tinsmithing, even in remote areas.

Continued respect and admiration for traditional arts, crafts and especially architecture is reflected in preservation efforts throughout the Southwest today. Many districts and buildings have been included in State and National Historic Registers, and there is an ongoing struggle to preserve old structures that have endured the ravages of a harsh environment, but might crumble in the wake of "progress."

Yet, in the face of technological advances, we have seen a reaffirmed commitment to building with adobe. There has been experimentation with styles and forms as well as with adobe itself. Developments include stabilized bricks (moisture-resistant adobes reinforced with a petroleum by-product), high-pressure earth ramming, and solar adaptations, both active and passive.

Many builders today, architects and nonarchitects alike, have discovered the attractions of using sun-baked earth. Adobe leaves much to individual imagination, though there are certain parameters within which traditional adobe architecture is most true to form. In the Southwest, a broad spectrum of new adobe buildings reflects the qualities inherent in this subtle and nondominating architectural form, and becomes part of its own enduring tradition.

Fort Lowell in Tucson, Arizona, was established in 1872 and occupied as a fort until 1891. Built in the Sonoran style of fired adobe bricks whitewashed with lime, the Fort has been restored to its original condition.

Fort Union, New Mexico, established by Lt. Col. Edwin Sumner in 1851. This compound was constructed in 1862 from local adobe bricks, milled lumber and fired brick. Fort Union had its own lumber mill and brickworks, as did most Territorial forts. Called the quintessential expression of Territorial architecture, Fort Union was the center of the new movement of Greek Revival style architecture in New Mexico. It now stands in ruins. *Photo ca. 1870, U.S. Army Signal Corps Collection in the Museum of New Mexico, neg number 1839.*

The Alvarado Hotel was built in 1902 in Albuquerque, New Mexico, by the Santa Fe Railroad in its new signature style called "mission revival." The Alvarado was designed by Charles Whittlesey and the adjacent Indian Building (the most popular stop) by Mary Colter. One of the outstanding examples of mission revival style, the Alvarado was destroyed in 1970. *Photo ca. 1905 by G. W. Hance, courtesy Museum of New Mexico, neg number 66003.*

The home of the Ilfeld family in Las Vegas, New Mexico, was built in the Territorial style made popular after the advent of the forts and the railroads. The Ilfelds were a wealthy merchant family who could afford the new materials and were familiar with the Eastern U.S. styles they strove to duplicate. *Photo ca. 1904, courtesy Museum of New Mexico, neg number 51874.*

The Montgomery Bell residence near Las Vegas, New Mexico. Mr. Bell was one of the early Black residents of New Mexico. He built this ranch house in the 1890s, in a mix of Eastern and New Mexican styles. *Photo by John C. Buchanan, courtesy Museum of New Mexico, neg number 14483.*

Three Artists — Three Cultures
Virginia Romero

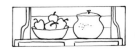

There is one *horno* (oven) in Taos Pueblo that no one uses for baking bread —the *horno* that Virginia Romero uses to fire her famous micaceous pottery. Now in her 90s, she made her first pot in 1919, remembering the traditional way her mother worked. She was always too busy actually to learn pottery making from her mother; Virginia did all the cooking for her nine siblings. "That's why they all like me so much!" she laughs. She did learn building from her mother, though. When a Spanish lady in Ranchos wanted a fireplace built, she called on Virginia's mother, Teodora Trujillo. Teodora took young Virginia along to help with the mud and adobe work. She learned well, applying her knowledge years later at the home of Millicent Rogers, now a museum in Taos. All of the adobe fireplaces and *bancos* there were built by Virginia, and she laid the adobe floor in the Hispanic Hall as well. In 1986 the Millicent Rogers Museum honored Virginia Romero with a retrospective show of her pottery. The earliest piece in the show was from 1919, the most recent was just fired and polished, dated 1986.

Mrs. Romero and her husband Joe, a former governor of Taos Pueblo, live in the summer house they built thirty years ago. Their winter house in the multi-storied pueblo complex is used on ceremonial days. Virginia built two *hornos* in her yard—one for baking bread and one for firing pottery. She gathers special clay from locations known to only a few potters, soaks it overnight in warm water, and then coils the shapes with her facile hand. After polishing with a special stone, the pot is fired with sheep dung in her *horno.*

Virginia's favorite designs are rain patterns and lizards, symbols of good luck. The other designs are, she says, "whatever you want them to be."

Virginia Romero holding one of her recent pots, and standing by her bread *horno*. The golden micacous jar has a cloud design.

Virginia Romero was for some time the only potter in Taos making bean pots and wedding vases in the old traditional way. This bean pot, *opposite, left,* is ready for use, and the pinto beans that are cooked in it will be especially delicious.

At the Millicent Rogers Museum, *opposite, right,* the adobe floor and stairs with flagstone risers built by Virginia Romero.

Traditional Taos Pueblo ceiling, *below, right.* The split cedar *latillas* have been whitewashed. In the early days, jaspé, a type of gypsum, would have been used; in this case, the white is paint. Note the elegant arched doorway.

Simple and elegant corner fireplace, *below,* built by Virginia Romero, in the Millicent Rogers Museum in Taos, New Mexico.

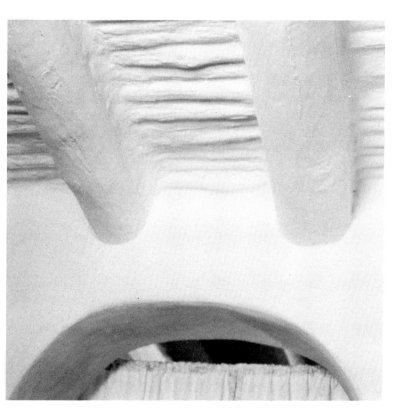

Virginia Romero modeled this fireplace in the Millicent Rogers Museum after the one in her summer home. The rope-carved chimney is unique, and she couldn't resist adding the lizard ceramic piece that offers good luck.

This row of five Indian baskets hangs in the Romero home in Taos Pueblo. The wicker design is from the Third Mesa Villages at Hopi.

Virginia's sister, Emily, and her husband, Eliseo Concha, built their fireplace together in 1935. Dark plaster surrounds the firepit. The Conchas have been active in many Taos Pueblo projects; Eliseo taught shop at the Pueblo school for twenty-seven years, and Emily worked at the clinic for seventeen years.

The walls in Teresa Archuleta-Sagel's studio are hand-plastered and polished *tierra amarilla*. Teresa was given a bucketful of this precious micaceous clay from a potter friend, and her mother taught her some of the traditional techniques of plaster preparation and application. As Madilde Garcia-Archuleta remembers, the process was for the men to *enjarrar* (put the rough coats of mud up), then the women would *alisar* (hand-rub the damp adobe to take the final cracks out). The job of *encalando* (applying the final slip or whitewash) was also left to the women, who often added a decorative *sanefa* (stencil design) to the walls as a final touch.

Teresa experimented when she prepared the final plaster slip. Some told her to screen the clay when dry, others to soak it overnight (soaking worked best for her); some said the best binder was Elmer's glue, others suggested powdered milk, and her mother offered flour paste, but Teresa found buttermilk worked best when mixed with the *tierra amarilla* clay.

The fireplace mantel, *lower right,* in the Sagel living room features a cedar Guadalupe by Benjamin Lopez, with carved leaves for rays. Also featured is Indian pottery from San Ildefonso and Santa Clara Pueblos. The jar in the center has a traditional shape, called a wedding vase. This one, made by Madeline Naranjo, has "Teresa" and "Jim" carved into the clay, with other traditional designs.

Three Artists — Three Cultures
Teresa Archuleta-Sagel

Growing up in Espanola, Teresa Archuleta-Sagel couldn't decide whether to be a weaver or a poet. "I married the poet, and began to weave in 1972," she writes. Teresa and her husband, Jim Sagel, live in an adobe home they built on the banks of the Rio Grande River. Teresa talks of the need for sharing community and family knowledge in the process of building and in her own art of weaving. Plastering, spinning and carding are often communal efforts, offering an occasion for sharing stories, techniques and time together. In contrast, Teresa's weavings are very personal statements. Though many of the design elements show influences passed down from generations of New Mexican, Mexican, Spanish and European forebears, Teresa incorporates them into her own vision. Each design and color is rooted in the landscape. Often inspiration comes from river walks and lightning storms. She likes to capture in her textiles what she calls "what the air looks like."

Teresa Archuleta-Sagel at her loom. She learned weaving with the guidance of Doña Agueda Martinez and Ruth Vigil, and she carries on the tradition of researching and using the old methods of gathering wild grasses and plants from the New Mexico mountains, valleys and deserts to use in dyeing her wools.

Teresa's father, Jacobo Archuleta, built Teresa's first loom—a four-harness traditional pedal loom. He also guided Jim in building their home. The trips to the family land in Coyote, New Mexico, to gather viga logs are the source of many fond memories and colorful stories. Here, Teresa stands with her father in front of his *corrales* by the Rio Grande River: the Sangre de Cristo Mountains are in the distance.

The bedroom fireplace, built in traditional corner style by Jacobo Archuleta, who built fireplaces for the Forest Service throughout Northern New Mexico.

View of the Pedernal to the south from the Ghost Ranch portal.

Memories of a last conversation with Georgia O'Keeffe, in Santa Fe:
Sandy: "Do you imagine you are at the ranch? Dream that you are walking out there?"
Miss O'Keeffe: "Yes. I dream that."
Sandy: "What about Texas, about your other travels? Do you go there much?"
Miss O'Keeffe: "No. To the ranch. Most of the time, the ranch."

Georgia O'Keeffe purchased her Ghost Ranch adobe house in 1940. She called it her "favorite place," referring both to the beloved house as well as to the setting, which deeply touched and affected her life.

Every summer morning at dawn she walked across the red hills towards the red, ochre and soft white cliffs behind the ranch. Evenings were spent on the portal facing the Pedernal. As the sun set, the late glow of warm red would spread across the sage. On moonlit nights the sage tops would shine and the sky's innumerable stars partially vanish.

The entryway to the Mabel Dodge Luhan estate in Taos. Huge cottonwoods shade the massive wooden gates set into sculpted adobe walls. Mabel Dodge Luhan was instrumental in introducing many famous artists and writers of the early twentieth century to the Southwest.

The Mabel Dodge Luhan house in Taos, now the Las Palomas Educational Retreat Center. In 1900 Mabel and her husband Tony Luhan, from Taos Pueblo, enlarged the original 200-year-old house into its present 22-room size, with lines and shapes that echo Taos Pueblo and Taos Mountain.

The Restaurante Rancho de Chimayo, near Santa Fe, is located in the family home built by Hermenegildo and Trinidad Jaramillo in the 1880s. The family has been in Chimayo since the 1700s and Arturo Jaramillo and his wife run the popular restaurant today.

The colors and textures of adobe are captured in this photograph of a traditional exterior. The plaster is mud and straw mixed and applied by hand.

Built in 1820, the Morada de Don Fernando de Taos served as a meeting place for the Penitente brotherhood, a religious group who provided guidance when the village was without a parish priest. In 1973 the two remaining members of the local morada transferred the building for preservation to the Kit Carson Foundation.

The San José de Gracia Church in the village of Las Trampas, New Mexico, was built between 1760 and 1776. The wooden bell towers and portal detailing are Gothic Revival Style, and the church features a hidden clerestory window to light the altar.

Standing almost a block long, this store building in Vallecitos, New Mexico, blazes its brightly painted portal posts. The original adobe building was covered with wood and metal fronting to modernize the store in the early 1930s.

A colorful fruit stand near Velarde, New Mexico, displays locally grown produce on the portal of an adobe home. Pumpkins, chiles, corn and many other fall fruits are popular crops in the rural areas of Northern New Mexico.

Opposite. Earth colors tint each surface in this room in the Minges' home. The floor is local mud mixed with oxblood; the mauve plaster comes from the hills near Cuba, New Mexico, and the light plaster color from the Sandia Mountains. Each color is prepared in a different way and applied by hand. The walls are cleaned by using a light solution of color on a paintbrush or rag.

A tile Guadalupe in an adobe wall. Flecks of straw catch the sunlight. Straw is added to the mud plaster to serve as a binder.

Designed by Art and Mark Adair of Taos, this bright casual kitchen combines both cooking and informal dining areas. The table is painted by Taos artist Jim Wagner.

Entrance to the patio of Georgia O'Keeffe's Abiquiu house. There has been a dwelling on this hill for as long as there have been people in the Abiquiu valley; Anasazi sites are abundant throughout the area. The Spanish part of the house was built in the 1700s by ancestors of Julian Chavez. Miss O'Keeffe bought the property (the house was being used as a pigpen) from the Catholic church in 1945. From a letter from Georgia O'Keeffe to J. O. Seth, December 4, 1945: "I have decided to take the Abiquiu place . . . If by any chance the property does not include the little place where the pigpen, chicken house and outhouse are, maybe for a little we could buy the small plot . . . of course all pigs are to be out."

While looking through old deeds they found that the house and property had been sold in 1826 for a bushel of corn, two cows, one with calf, and a serape.

Georgia O'Keeffe on the portal of the Ghost Ranch house with Bobo, her black chow, beside her. *Photograph entitled "Georgia O'Keeffe, Ghost Ranch 1975" © by Dan Budnik.*

Two views within the entry patio of the Abiquiu house, a patio that was the subject of more than twenty paintings from 1946 to 1960. Miss O'Keeffe's attraction to the stark, simple and elegant shape of the doors against the expanse of adobe wall was the major reason she bought the house, *top. Below,* her sculpture on the old well house lid.

The "unroofed room" off the dining room at the "big house," the Abiquiu house.
She had always talked of covering this with sliding glass panels, which would
permit it to be completely open in the summer and still light in winter. On the
table sits the model for the huge sculpture currently in the Museum of Modern
Art, San Francisco.

Fireplace in the Abiquiu house dining room.

Deep adobe *nicho* with rocks in the north wall of the dining room.

Living room at the Abiquiu house.

Of the sparcity of furnishings and uncluttered walls so typical of both houses, she said that she liked to have empty walls, that she liked a space to think in. If there is too much on the walls, there is less chance something new will enter your mind, and, fittingly, "There is nothing more beautiful than a white canvas. Nothing on it but the first white. Anything you add after that is never as good." (1965).

Earth walls, earth floors, mud plaster were not only the sensible choices at the time of renovation because the native people could build with earth so beautifully, had done for hundreds of years, but they were *the* aesthetic choice for Miss O'Keeffe. There is a feeling living in a house made of the earth which cannot be duplicated in any other material. She didn't ever define it, "words aren't much good. You just have to feel it." She said of the Abiquiu house, that she never tried to make it look Indian or Spanish, that she just wanted it to be her house with what she liked around her.

Regarding her adobe floor, she said, "I wanted an adobe floor and we worked for weeks to get it right. I don't know why women don't wear sensible shoes. Before I've caught them, they've come in here in high heels making little holes like chickens pecking. Then we have to patch everywhere." With her usual subtle humor, she added, "That's not the only reason people should wear sensible shoes."

Two views from the garden of the Abiquiu house. Miss O'Keeffe's garden yielded quarts and quarts of raspberries, which she gave to friends and which were stowed for winter desserts in freezers in both Abiquiu and Ghost Ranch. Fresh vegetables, which she also loved, were in abundance.

An Alexander Calder mobile, once beside her bed at Ghost Ranch, hangs beside the simple adobe fireplace. The walls and *bancos* are finished a *tierra bayita* (light tan) mud plaster. The ceiling is split cedar; the floors adobe. A Juan Hamilton bronze sculpture sits to the right of the fireplace.

A doorway from the entry patio leading past a guest bedroom into another courtyard and to the studio.

Entrance to the separate studio and bedroom, former outbuildings and stables, which local Abiquiu people helped her to rebuild.

A simple hooded fireplace in Miss O'Keeffe's Abiquiu bedroom. Peeled aspen *latillas* span the vigas for the ceiling, and the walls and floor are earth. Large windows overlook the fields and the Chama river below. One of her unfinished clay pots sits beside the fireplace. About the large studio room, adjacent bedroom and bath, she said "This would be enough. Big enough. Almost everything I need is here."

She also often mentioned that the perfect house would be something small and simple, a big, open room. "If I built again, I would do that, and it would be enough."

Bone and rocks on a narrow adobe shelf above Miss O'Keeffe's bed, Abiquiu.

Array of smooth rocks beside a rattlesnake skeleton inset into an adobe *banco*, Abiquiu living room.

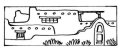

Pueblo Style Exteriors

Looking at a Pueblo-style building, one is struck by two things—the softness of line in the contoured walls and the gentleness of earth colors on the surfaces. Pueblo style generally defines a style that is solid and round-edged with irregular walls. A Pueblo-style building can be either one story or more, and often has stepped levels. They are always flat-roofed, and usually a rounded cap at the top of the wall extends a foot or more above roof level to serve as a fire wall. Door and window openings are deep, the fenestration simple.

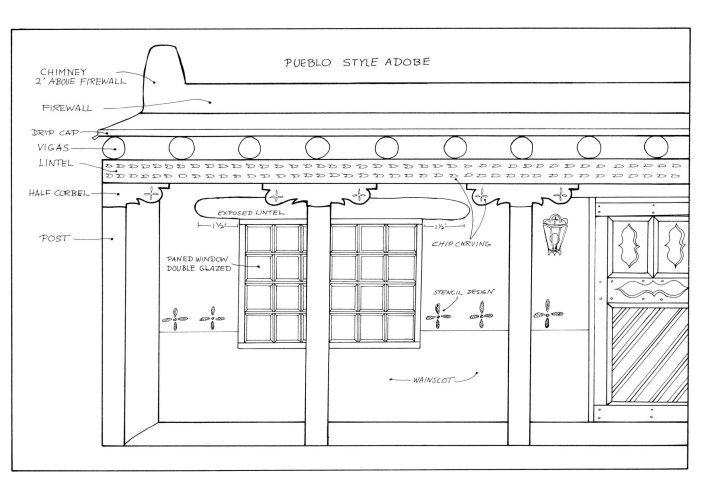

The sculptural quality of adobe is typified in this multilevel home. A gently sloping wall follows the contour of the land, enclosing a large fenced front garden. Taos Mountain, the sacred mountain of the Taos Pueblo people, rises snowcapped in the distance.

The first story of this multilevel pueblo-style home was part of the "Plaza Vieja," the original walled town of Ranchos de Taos. The top stories were added in the late 1940s and feature large south-facing windows. The house is now owned by Sally Kugel.

This private chapel is one of many buildings constructed on a large Santa Fe estate in the 1920s. The exterior is modeled after a Spanish mission church, with large carved doors and a bell tower set into the impressive adobe facade.

Once part of the famous Mabel Dodge Luhan complex, this multistoried adobe strongly reflects the influence of the buildings of Taos Pueblo in its curved lines and rounded shapes.

This modern pueblo revival-style adobe sits nestled in the piñon-dotted foothills near Santa Fe. Its color and simple soft lines blend nicely with the surrounding landscape.

Though not built of adobe, the Fine Arts Museum on the plaza in Santa Fe was one of the major influences in pueblo-revival architectural style. Built in 1917, the Museum was a copy of the New Mexico building from the San Diego Exposition and was modeled after the Acoma Mission church.

An example of a modern adaptation of the simple one-story pueblo style. Low-lying homes are reminiscent of early Spanish ranch homes.

This Taos exterior, near the La Loma Historic District in Taos, is a blend of Territorial and pueblo styles. The fenestration is largely Territorial, while the second-story open portal is in more pueblo style.

The Hughston home in Taos, with a bank of small-paned south-facing windows. The portal treatment is unusual because the support poles have been plastered. Note the traditional Territorial-style door.

Also part of the Mabel Dodge Luhan complex, this sculpted adobe home abounds in organic shapes and curvilinear forms.

Left, the Mission of the Sun, a chapel built in 1952 by the well-known artist Ted DeGrazia. Sited in the saguaro-laden foothills near Tucson, Arizona, this adobe home is a unique personal statement. *Right*, this modest, low-lying pueblo-style adobe was built in the 1930s by artist Homer Boss and his wife, Suzanne, near the site of an Indian ruin in Quarteles, New Mexico.

The Santa Fe River runs beside many adobe homes in downtown Santa Fe. Here, icicles form on a small granite waterfall on Alameda Street.

Territorial Style Exteriors

   Decorative wood trim is the outstanding feature of a Territorial-style adobe. The trim adorns portals, doors, window frames and, occasionally, a second-story balcony. There are traditionally two types of Territorial buildings in the Southwest. The flat-roofed building of one or two stories with brick coping at the top of the walls is seen throughout the Southwest. The pitched roof mountain style, perhaps equally as old, developed as a folk-style adaptation in colder regions where snow accumulations made flat-roofed structures impractical. Traditionally, the pitch of the roof depends on the proportions of available materials, especially the length of roofing timbers.

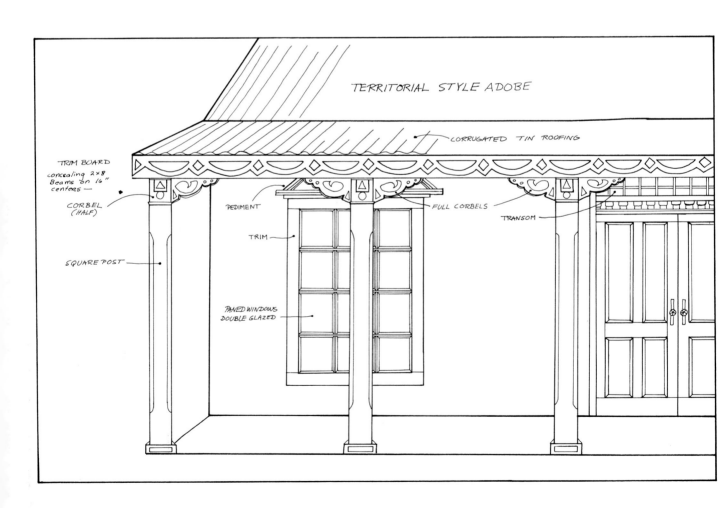

TERRITORIAL STYLE ADOBE

CORRUGATED TIN ROOFING

TRIM BOARD
concealing 2×8
Beams on 16"
centers —

CORBEL
(HALF)

PEDIMENT

FULL CORBELS

TRANSOM

TRIM

SQUARE POST

PANED WINDOWS
DOUBLE GLAZED

A fine example of a Northern New Mexico Territorial home. This pitched roof adobe with dormer windows and a south-facing porch sits on a hill above the farm land and *acequias* (irrigation ditches). Houses like this one grew as the family grew; in this example, the addition on the right mirrors the original structure.

The Casa de la Abuelita (Grandmother's House) at Rancho de las Golondrinas. This small mountain-style home was a typical structure in Northern New Mexico in the early 1900s. The grandmother of the family (and a grandchild or two) lived near the main house and tended a small herb garden. The pitched roof is constructed of hand-cut wood, as is the small well covering.

This large family home in El Rito, New Mexico, is a striking example of Territorial-style architecture. Built in a large square, it features a second-story portal the length of the south side.

Traditional L-shaped mountain Territorial home in Northern New Mexico. The narrow portal, tin roof and wood trim detailing are all distinctive elements of this style.

Juan Hamilton's home and studio in Abiquiu, New Mexico, is an example of a successful modern adaptation of the Territorial-style vocabulary. His studio upstairs takes advantage of the north light, and the interior is simple and open.

In the 1700s the Cordovas family of Taos Valley built this mill on the Rio Pueblo south of the Taos Plaza. In 1952 Otto Mears Pitcher retained the simple mud exterior and classic lines of the original structure in his sensitive remodeling.

Named "El Zaguán" for its covered corridor leading to the courtyard from the street, this Santa Fe landmark epitomizes the flat-roofed Territorial style. Originally a four-room pueblo-style home, it was converted and enlarged in 1849 when the brick coping and Territorial-style wood sash windows were added.

The Epifano and Adelaida Jaramillo home was built in Chimayo in 1884 by Epifano and his brother, Hermenegildo. Today, it is a bed and breakfast inn featuring guest rooms decorated with turn of the century antiques. Hanging from the roof are *ristras* (strings) of locally grown chiles.

In the towns of Arizona and Northern Sonora, typical traditional homes front unassumingly on the street, with few windows. Only massive carved gates give a hint of the interior courtyard area. Ranch houses, scattered throughout the area, were simple adobe structures with straight lines and square or rectangular floor plans.

The home of Virginia Barnes in the foothills north of Scottsdale was designed by artist and builder Bill Tull of Phoenix. This desert-adapted home features Moorish windows and doors and a Sonoran-style straight-lined, exposed adobe exterior.

The Belloli home on Upper Canyon Road in Santa Fe is distinctly Mission style in detail and design. The tile roof, whitewashed walls and carved stone window openings, so common in Arizona, California, Texas and Northern Mexico, are unusual in Santa Fe.

A drawing of Mesa Verde, a prehistoric Indian cliff dwelling that was occupied from about 400 to 1200 A.D. Most sites from this period were oriented to take maximum advantage of the sun. Other large pueblos were often arranged in a large semicircle facing south, with massive heat-retaining walls to absorb the sunlight.

Closeup view of a passive solar greenhouse in Taos. Large thermopane windows face south, and a brick floor absorbs and retains the heat.

Direct-gain passive-solar adobe built by Rod Goebel. This view from the patio shows the large angled second-story windows.

Passive-solar Territorial-style adobe in Taos. A greenhouse extends along the entire south side, providing heat for adjacent rooms. Adobe walls are effective heat "sinks," radiating warmth for several cloudy days.

This Santa Fe solar home takes advantage of the many sunny winter days in New Mexico to heat the interior. The angle of the windows has been carefully calculated for this latitude. Well-insulated passive-solar adobes are remarkably warm in winter, requiring very little supplementary heat.

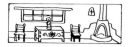

Interiors

The interiors of early Native American dwellings were extremely functional and simple. A rooftop ladder led into a small square room with polished earth floors. A firepit warmed the room, the smoke escaping through a hole in the fragrant cedar or willow ceiling. Wood beams were covered with brush and layered with an earthen roof. Poles for hanging clothes or other belongings lined whitewashed walls; hand-coiled and painted pots for storing grains and other staples were placed in cool corners; sleeping mats of fur or woven reed lay on the floor or were rolled up for seating.

By the mid-eighteenth century, interiors incorporated many Spanish architectural introductions. Ground-level doors provided new access, and window openings were slightly enlarged and protected by wooden bars. Adobe fireplaces with chimneys were built to warm each room. Furnishings included wool sleeping mats and floor coverings, chairs, chests and built-in cabinets, called *alacenas*. Woodwork was simply carved and often decorated with powdered earth pigments in a variety of soft hues. Usually a room was 15 feet wide, which was the span of a good viga log. Pine or fir viga beams were combined with aspen or cedar crosspieces, called *latillas*, to form patterned and textured ceilings similar to those of the Indians. The only light came from small high windows sometimes glazed with mica or selenite, and from the fires in the corner fireplaces. Candles were scarce and were saved for special or religious occasions.

Anglo settlers made many changes in interior spaces, especially after the establishment of the railroad in 1880. Room uses became specialized when beds, couches and cast-iron stoves arrived from the East. One of the most popular new materials, glass, soon replaced mica. As defensibility became less of a factor, small windows gave way to larger, and there was more interior light. Milled lumber allowed for standardization in door and window openings. Wood was also used for floors, wainscoting and, as in the case of Territorial fireplace mantels, sometimes purely for decoration.

Opposite, top. Combination kitchen, bath, living and dining areas, 18 x 32 feet, 14-inch-thick adobe walls. Flat wall fireplace with *padercita* and *banco*, 10-foot bookshelf inset into adobe wall. Support beams and lintel 6 x 10 inches are concealed by mud plaster. *Middle.* Traditional New Mexican bedroom, 15 x 22 feet. High fireplace with wood storage below. Wood spindled *trastero* incorporated a dressing table. Equipale (pigskin and cedar) furniture from Mexico, Spanish Colonial trunks and carved headboards, Navajo rugs. *Bottom.* Pueblo-style interior (Las Cruces) with high ceilings. Flat spindle balcony in Territorial style. Chip-carved pine furniture from Patzcuaro, Mexico. Kitchen/living room, 15 x 36 feet.

Interior view of the Fremont House in Tucson, Arizona. The original house was built in 1858 by José Maria Sosa. John Fremont, who was the fifth Territorial governor of Arizona, probably occupied this house in 1881. The carrizo, or cane, ceiling was typical in the Arizona-Sonora area.

The famous guide and trapper, Kit Carson, lived in this house with his wife, Josefa Jaramillo, from 1842 until his death in 1868. The twelve-room home is now owned by the Kit Carson Foundation. The furniture is mostly original, and was brought over the Santa Fe Trail in the 1850s.

Opposite, the sala or main formal room in the home of Ward Alan and Shirley Minge. Details and furnishings in this room are exactly as they would have been in the eighteenth century, with only the latter-day addition of the Territorial-style door at the far end of the room. Note the flagstone floor, the finely carved corbels on the vigas (roof beams) and the simple tin candle sconces.

Traditional Indian paintings and W.P.A.-era furnishings decorate this adobe originally buil in 1797, and remodeled in 1919 by the famou Taos artist Ernest L. Blumenschein. Blumer schein was sent west by the Santa Fe Railroa Company to paint Indians, and stayed in Tac to help found the Taos Art Colony.

Spanish Colonial carvings, or santos, *top righ* cover the end wall of this Territorial-style sal. Depictions of Catholic saints, santos and fla painted retablos are popular images througho the Southwest. A fine colcha (a tradition. Spanish embroidery) covers the television an stereo, and Rio Grande weavings (textiles wove in Northern New Mexico from the 1700s o adorn the floor-level panels of the santo wa.

Antique Italian and Spanish furniture, *righ* complements the traditional adobe interior this eighteenth-century Santa Fe home. Th room is long and narrow, built with vigas broug down from the mountains above Santa Fe.

Mr. and Mrs. John B. Arhen's sitting room the La Loma Historical District of Taos cente around a traditional corner fireplace with ste ped wall and *banco* (seating bench built in the wall). Note the large Taos Pueblo cotto wood drum.

73

The focus of this Taos living room is the fireplace built into a stepped wall with *banco* seating areas and decorative *nichos* on either side. Owners and designers Mark and Art Adair own the Clay and Fiber gallery in Taos, and their home reflects their interest in folk art and contemporary crafts.

Ponderosa beams painted with Navajo symbols span the ceiling of this living room in Phoenix, Arizona. Roof boards and beams are uneven because most of the wood was used for the war effort when this house was built in 1926. A Hopi kachina, carved to represent one of the Hopi gods or spirits, sits on the side table in the foreground.

The home of Oliver and Jean Seth was the second home to be built on the northern outskirts of Santa Fe in 1929. This large room features a flat wall fireplace and 30-foot-high ceilings. A huge mirror reflects much of the room. French doors open into the sunroom and the south-facing portal.

Two views of the living room in the Arnold and Elaine Horwitch home in Santa Fe. Contemporary paintings, Indian pottery and weavings, and a tooled leather saddle lend a strong Southwestern flavor to this modern traditional interior.

The living room of well-known folk art collectors, Alexander and Susan Girard, reflects their interest in folk art. The central *banco* area is decorated with special pieces from India, Africa and Mexico, and faces an unusual built-in fireplace. A carved wooden bird peers out of the wall in a curve of the coved ceiling.

This Arizona interior of whitewashed Queen Creek adobes (fired bricks or mud from the Queen Creek River near Phoenix) is decorated with paintings by the Taos Colony of artists. A Hennings hangs over the fireplace, and Gaspard, Couse, Berninghaus, Ufer and Fechin paintings line the walls. A bronze sculpture by Henry Moore rests before the fireplace.

Sunlight streams through saguaro shutters and floor-to-ceiling windows in designer Bill Tull's living room in Phoenix. The domed ceiling and arched doorway reflect the Moorish influences he successfully incorporates into his Arizona adobes.

In the 1830s, open shelves and hanging herbs and spices were both decorative and functional. This room, in the Martinez Hacienda near Taos, is dominated by a shepherd's fireplace, which functioned as a heating and cooking area. The shelf area above was used for sleeping, and for drying herbs and other staples.

The 1850s kitchen in the Kit Carson home in Taos also features open shelves. By this time the room use was specialized, and only cooking and food preparation took place here. The large glass Territorial windows were added after the arrival of the railroad trade in the 1880s.

Two views of the kitchen area in the Horwitch home in Santa Fe. Skylights and south windows brighten this country kitchen and breakfast room. Southwestern details can be seen in the coved ceiling, the corbeled hood over the stove, and the corner fireplace painted with Indian pottery designs.

The dining room of the Gerald Peters home in Santa Fe. Furnishings include an antique Spanish Colonial table, chest and shelves, probably dating from the 1820s. A Mexican tin chandelier hangs from the chip-carved beams, and a Georgia O'Keeffe painting, one of her black cross series, graces the far wall.

A dining room in Taos with a traditional country feeling. Note the carved hutch from Patzcuaro, Mexico, and the iron light fixture and files, also from Mexico. The adobe walls are plastered with local mud, mixed with straw and sand, and applied by hand.

Dining room in the original part of the de la Peña home in Santa Fe, constructed by 1845. The 3-foot-thick adobe walls can be seen in the window opening at left. The large cupboard has the date 1660 carved on the right-hand door. Atop it rest a Chemehueri basket from the 1800s and a contemporary sculpture by Juan Hamilton.

When this home was built around 1910, this long narrow room served as a small private chapel. Now a formal dining room, the chapel area is visible at the far end of the room. The dining table and chairs rest on a large Navajo rug from the Two Grey Hills area of Arizona.

A country kitchen in Nambe, New Mexico, with hand-adzed beams and a tiled alcove for the gas stove. The tile doorway to the right leads to the breakfast area. *Right*, this sculpted adobe stove hood is a creative alternative to standard vents. Mexican tiles adorn the counters and the wall.

The Berninghaus home, *opposite below,* now the residence of Mr. and Mrs. Robert Daughters, includes this semiformal dining room with traditional New Mexican elements such as the built-in *alacena* (cupboard) and Indian-style fireplace.

Virginia Barnes' sunny Arizona kitchen features copper cabinets, which disguise the refrigerator and shelves. A convenient central work area adds counter space.

Located in downtown Phoenix, this traditional adobe home includes a formal dining room with Mexican tile floors and hand-hewn beams. The Spanish-style fireplace is from the Earl of Plymouth's home in England and becomes part of this well-blended eclectic style.

Designed by architect Victor Viramontes, this kitchen in the Johnson home in Taos incorporates multiple work and seating areas. Note the hand-carved wooden cabinets and doors by local craftsmen Greg Kaslo and Paul Neveu.

Jean and Oliver Seth's dining room in Santa Fe. The spindled screen, carved by Volker de la Harpe, opens or closes to separate the kitchen and dining areas. The corner fireplace is built specially into a small stepped wall called a *padercita*. The pumpkin-shaped glass light and tile floor are Mexican.

Whitewashed walls and ceiling help to reflect the light in this Taos bedroom. Victorian furnishings complement the traditional pueblo-style interior. Note the distinctive arched doorway.

Thomas Jefferson inspired this alcove bed designed by Kristina Wilson and
Sandy Seth, which is built into the wall of this pueblo-style room. The entire
room was hand-built by Sandy Seth, including the traditional corner fireplace
(detailed in the fireplace chapter). Note the folk-style trim around the windows
and the "Penasco"-style panels that cover the storage area under the bed. The
floor is earth, covered with Navajo, Oriental and Rio Grande rugs.

View through the wide-
arched entry into the bedroom of a traditional pueblo-
style adobe in the La Loma
Historic District of Taos. A
corner fireplace is built on a
high hearth to radiate heat
towards the beds.

This turn-of-the-century-style bedroom is in a traditional Territorial-style home in Nambe, New Mexico. A built-in *alacena* (cabinet) near the antique brass bed provides some storage area. (There were never closets in early southwestern homes.)

Bedroom in the Ernest Blumenschein home on La Loma in Taos. Note the beautifully proportioned corner fireplace with decorative stepped walls on either side. Ernest and his wife, Mary Greene Shepard, renovated and expanded the original home, which dated from 1797. Their daughter, Helen Blumenschein, gave the eleven-room adobe to the Kit Carson Foundation in Taos.

Mexican shuttered windows are the distinctive features in this Mexican Colonial-style home in the Catalina foothills near Tucson.

A Moorish arch in deep adobe walls frames this view of the bathroom in the Bill Tull home in Phoenix. Full-sized saguaro shutters open onto a south-facing patio. The antique tub faces a small fireplace.

Top, hand-painted Mexican tile steps lead to the circular bathtub lit by a domed skylight. Phoenix craftsmen created the colorful stained-glass window.

Top right, this bath in Santa Fe features a green glazed-tile tub and Mexican tile floors. A stepped wall separates the dressing room from the bath, and a skylight set between the vigas lights both areas.

Hand-carved cabinets and wood details by Taos craftsman Philip Martinez decorate the master bath in the Johnson home in Taos. A partial wall set with turned spindles separates the toilet from the rest of the room.

Small conference area in a Santa Fe study. An unusual early altarpiece surrounds the fireplace, and Mexican leather chairs are gathered around a Taos deerhide and cottonwood drum.

90

A handmade bench of Spanish Colonial design is used in the entryway to store boots and other items. Navajo rugs, a stone-carved depiction of the Virgin of Guadalupe, and a Penasco-style door set a traditional mood in this Taos adobe.

The sitting room of Edwin Bewley's home in Taos with a traditional corner fireplace and adobe *banco.* Part of a collection of fine early Spanish Colonial retablos and a group of straw inlay crosses decorate the walls.

Moorish-style dome with skylights and ceiling fan forms the ceiling in this Phoenix home designed by Bill Tull.

Two views of the studio of sculptor Juan Hamilton in Tesuque, New Mexico. Hamilton designed the building in elegant and simple style. The floors are highly polished to complement his bronze and lacquered sculptural shapes. Deep-set windows run the entire length of the studio to allow natural light to enter and to provide a view of the Tesuque countryside.

This long entry hall connects the living room and the formal dining room and features tile floors, squared ceiling beams, Mexican tin light fixtures and Navajo rugs.

Hallway of Moorish-style *nichos* with an Indian pot in each. The star pattern on the door is mirrored on each door in the entry hall.

Studio of Valerie Graves, a Taos artist. Painting props of horse bridles and other riding gear hang from the easel. Two skylights cut into the herringbone-patterned ceiling provide extra light. An adobe corner fireplace faces the main working area.

This greenhouse in the Adair home in Taos helps heat the kitchen, dining room and master bedroom. The brick floor absorbs daytime heat, as does the adobe wall between the greenhouse and other rooms, radiating stored heat at night. The winter sun comes about 12 feet into the room while the 1 1/2-foot roof overhang outside prevents overheating in the summer months.

A converted zaguán, now a greenhouse in a large Territorial home in Nambe. Vines cover the viga ceiling, and the floor is constructed of pen tiles (bricks made at the Penitentiary of New Mexico in the 1940s). The many-paned small windows create a more traditional feeling than do larger expanses of glass.

Walls, Bancos and Nichos

On a traditional adobe home, it is the soft earth plaster laced with straw one sees first. Inside, the colors and textures reflect and enhance the clear southwestern light.

In his 1630 memoirs, Fray Alonso de Benavides described the process of adobe wall building in some of the mission churches in New Mexico. He writes that the custom was for the women and children to build the walls, while men looked down on this, and spent their time hunting, spinning, weaving and at carpentry.

Once the walls were completed, the complex and critical aspect of adobe work began—plastering. Traditionally, Hispanic and Indian men mixed the mud with organic binders (usually straw) and a little sand, and the women *enjarradoras* (plasterers) laid the first and second rough coats of plaster. When still damp, the last layer was smoothed on by hand by the women. The finish coat, or slip, was pure earth, finely screened, mixed to a soupy consistency and applied with sheepskin, brush, sponge or hand.

Plaster and slip colors are natural earth tones from stones, clay and minerals. The secrets of gathering and processing this earth were passed on from generation to generation and are still valuable lore. The most commonly used color, *tierra blanca*, is a whitewash or jaspé of native micaceous gypsum, which is baked, pulverized, and mixed with water and flour. This light color maximizes light reflection and was often used in churches where it glittered in the candlelight. Because jaspé easily brushed off on clothes, a darker plaster slip or protective cloth covered the walls about two feet above the floor, forming a dado.

Tierra azul, a rare and lovely blue; *tierra amarilla*, a micaceous yellow or tan; and many other shades of green, mauve, purple and blue from the sandstone and clay layers of the southwestern desert were also used, traditionally to highlight *nichos*, windows or doors, and for stencil designs and decorative molding.

Carved and incised plaster decoration is most common in the Sonoran desert areas of the Southwest. Exquisite examples can be seen at the San Xavier church near Tucson. There are also remnants of carved plaster in the prehistoric ruins in Aztec, New Mexico.

Opposite, top row. Stepped *padercita*, *nicho* and *banco*. Prehistoric petroglyph designs. Raised mud plaster *tablita* surrounding *nicho*. *Second row.* Cloud *nicho* with natural earth motif. Incised arrangement. Detail of wall stencil with natural earth plasters. *Third row.* Incised arch *nicho* and oval *nicho* with stencil. Conch shell *nicho*, cottonwood santo by Orilinga and Eugencia Lopez, Cordova, New Mexico. Incised *nicho* design. *Bottom row.* Incised cross *nicho*. Scalloped wall recess with Guadalupe by Frank Brito, Santa Fe. *Padercita* with matching stepped *banco*.

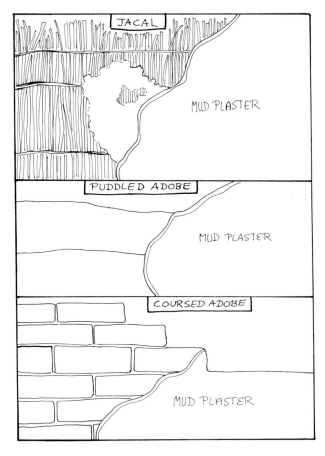

This drawing illustrates three common building methods in the Southwest.

Jacal, or wattle and daub construction, consists of upright poles bonded with mud chinking and plaster.

Puddled adobe buildings are made in successive hand-packed layers of damp mud that is left to dry between courses.

Adobe bricks are made in a wooden mold. Mud and binders are formed in the mold, and then left to dry in the sun. Adobes are laid like bricks during construction.

The oval *nichos* are carved into a thick adobe wall beside a traditional corner fireplace. Plastered shelves hold pottery animals from the Indian pueblos along the Rio Grande.

Cement plaster, introduced after 1880, seemed to be a simple answer to the need for replastering adobe walls every two years. Cement, however, does not adhere to adobe well, and when inevitable cracks occur, moisture becomes trapped inside the plaster shell, melting the adobe. It is said that adobe needs "to breathe." Cement plaster does not allow for this. One solution has been to plaster only the exterior walls with cement, allowing the interior walls to breathe. Another solution is the use of stabilized plaster (asphalt bitumen, a petroleum product), which can double the time between replasterings. However, the best solution is mud on mud, as it is the most practical for the adobe and the most grateful to the eye.

Built of hand-hewn beams mortared and plastered with mud, this storeroom at Rancho de las Golondrinas is an example of a typical seventeenth-century mountain shelter.

This adobe wall with decorative stone facing forms the north wall of the *placita* area at Rancho de las Golondrinas. Stone-faced buttresses support the long wall and frame the double wood doors. A wood transom above the door allows south light into the sala and chapel area. Millstones made of volcanic stone from the Jemez foothills lean against the buttresses.

An Indian couple from Jemez Pueblo work together to form adobe bricks in wooden forms. The man is mixing mud, clay, sand and straw, while the woman hand-packs the mud in the form. *Photo August 24, 1936, courtesy Museum of New Mexico, neg number 41588.*

Rows of bricks lie covered to dry and cure in the air. The man in the foreground uses a four-brick framework to mold the adobe bricks. *Photo courtesy Museum of New Mexico, neg number 40620.*

Adobe brick walls are laid in alternating courses and tied together at the corners with interlocking adobes. On this page are two examples of mud-plastered adobe walls, and a detail of Sandy Seth plastering an interior wall with a first coat of mud.

Bill Tull's Phoenix-style home. The exposed wall was built of stabilized adobe and then coated with a thin wash of cement and mud. Homes in the drier desert regions of Arizona and Northern Mexico are often unplastered because there is little rainfall to damage the exposed bricks.

This interior wall is built of Queen Creek fired adobe bricks, whitewashed and painted to preserve the brick texture. Note the large black olla by Margaret Tafoya of Santa Clara Pueblo and two historic Zia Pueblo jars.

A wall of exposed adobe bricks, Taos.

Two Indian women replaster an adobe wall, applying the mud by hand. *Photo, Sandoval County, New Mexico, October 16, 1936, courtesy Museum of New Mexico, neg number 41589.*

These two photographs show the group effort that goes into replastering a home. A woman pulls a bucket loaded with mud to the roof to replaster the firewall. Below, a new load of mud is dumped on the ground while a group of women plaster the wall; a hand applies the mud more forcefully and evenly than a trowel. *Photos by Mildred Crews, courtesy Museum of New Mexico, neg numbers 66644 and 66645.*

This doorway and wall at Rancho de Las Golondrinas is stenciled with a flower pattern and the wainscot is painted with a scallop design. The door and patterns are typical of the Territorial period in Northern New Mexico. *Top right,* a dark *tierra amarilla,* from clay deposits near Placitas, New Mexico, is used for this stencil design. The bird motif is from a Zia pot in the collection of Ward Alan Minge. An eighteenth-century retablo of San Antonio painted with earth pigments hangs above the *sanefa* (stencil). *Below left,* mural paintings of southwestern scenes surround the corner fireplace in the dining room of the Horwitch home in Santa Fe. *Below right,* interior and exterior wall painting is an old folk tradition throughout the Southwest; often the designs are religious or, as in this case, a decorative floral pattern. Lynn Garlick painted this folk design of partridge and pears on this doorway in Taos.

The baroque facade of the mission church of San Xavier del Bac near Tucson, Arizona. The entire surface is adorned with carved and molded plaster ornamentation. Established by Father Eusebio Kino in 1700, the building was complete by 1797, and remains an active parish church.

Two *nichos* in the San Xavier church feature elaborate carved and painted ornamentation of Spanish, Moorish and European origin brought to the New World by the Spanish. Local Indians painted these designs, and added their own elements as well. The Smithsonian is credited with identifying the sources of many of the colors used—red from ocotillo root, blue from saguaro sap, yellow from Palo Verde bark, green from sage and black from mesquite beans.

This *nicho* was specially designed for the carved wooden virgin, and features a carved wooden base.

Cross *nicho* and cross, designed by Alexander Girard.

This plaster *nicho* with brick roof trim is in the patio of the Fremont house in Tucson. A stone carving of the Virgin of Guadalupe sits inside the *nicho*.

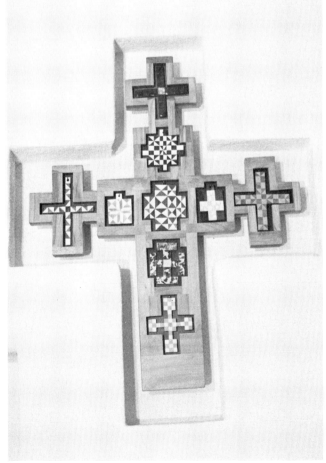

107

Nicho in Tucson, Arizona, holds special objects, and is decorated around the arch with pottery birds from Mexico. Also note the adobe wall shaped around the tree.

A step-arched *nicho* echos the wooden framework around this carving of Santo Niño de Atocha.

Bell *nicho* trimmed with carved stone from Mexico.

A Guadalupe by Frank Brito of Santa Fe rests in this traditional arch-shaped *nicho* sculpted in mud plaster.

Mexican stone carving of the sun, set into the wall as a decorative element.

Stone carving from Mexico is set into the exterior plaster of mud and straw.

Adobe *bancos* have evolved from being the only furniture in early Colonial homes and in the kivas (religious structures) of the Pueblos. They are now used as sculptural elements as well as for seating.

This simple *banco* is at Rancho de las Golondrinas. Plows and other farm equipment hang on the stone-faced adobe wall.

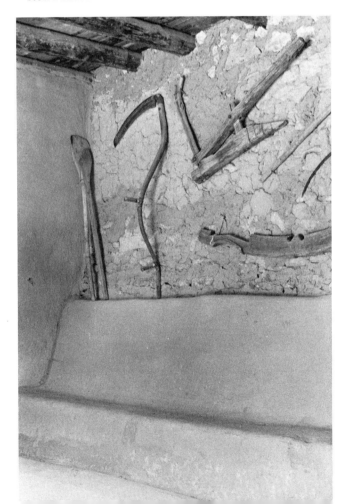

A series of decorative buttresses at the studio of Juan Hamilton in Tesuque.

Buttresses are primarily structural, though sometimes added as a decorative element to break the length of wall visually. If adobe corners are not well bonded, or if they become weak, a buttress is built to prevent the corner from separating, or the wall from leaning out.

Opposite, top left. Buttresses shore up a long adobe wall in Arizona.

Opposite, top right. A tall rounded buttress is built onto this high-walled Pueblo-style home in Taos.

Opposite, below. At the Islamic mosque in Abiquiu, New Mexico, rectangular shapes are built against the wall to act as buttresses.

Below left. A buttress and decorative corbel from the former El Conquistador Hotel in Tucson.

Below. Corner buttress at Las Palomas built to reinforce a weak wall.

111

Ceilings

Ceilings in the Southwest have changed little through time. Early Indians used available timber thatched with small shoots, reeds or weeds and roofed with layers of earth to insulate and protect the rooms from the weather. Ceilings in the Spanish period were the same, though metal tools allowed for some shaping of the wood. Vigas were left round or could be roughly squared, and lengths could be split with an axe. Anglo trade brought rapid changes with the arrival of sawn lumber, pressed tin and cheap muslin. Cloth, called *manta de techo* (ceiling cloth) was stretched across the ceiling and sometimes painted with flour and water, which dried to resemble a plaster ceiling. Cloth ceilings also served to insulate the room and catch the dust that sifted down between the *latillas.*

In traditional adobe homes vigas are most often spruce or fir. *Latillas* or *savinos* (small saplings laid across the vigas to form the ceiling) are usually aspen, split cedar, willow or, in Arizona, ocotillo, saguaro or carrizo (cane). Sawn boards of cedar, fir or pine are used to span the vigas in some homes. A coved ceiling is formed when the areas between the vigas are plastered to form a curved surface. Vigas or beams are sometimes supported by decorative carved corbels.

Each ceiling has a particular texture and pattern. Aromatic split cedar spans the vigas in a herringbone pattern in some while, in others, white aspen is laid between huge round fir beams.

Squared beams, pine *tablas* and carved corbel brackets in the Nicolai Fechin home in Taos.

Narrow aspen *latillas* are laid diagonally across squared beams in the home of Dr. and Mrs. Albert Simms in Santa Fe. The painted glass and tin light is from Mexico.

Opposite, top. Cane (carrizo) ceiling, Arizona. Aspen *latillas* in herringbone pattern. Pine boards *(tablas)* 1 inch x 8 inches, on chip-carved beams. *Middle.* Red fir *tablas,* 1 inch x 8 inches. Hand-split cedar. Herringbone pattern ocotillo, Arizona. *Bottom.* Hand-painted designs of Mimbres origin on white plaster (designed by Valerie Graves, Taos). Red willow star and circles tied over a background of gray willow (designed by Pancho Chacon, Arroyo Hondo). Plaster coved ceiling.

An unusual method of securing vigas with rawhide strips on the portal in the Fremont house in Tucson.

Close-up of the corbel carvings in the ceiling.

The sala in the Minge home near Albuquerque features a 20-foot-high ceiling of rounded vigas and split cedar *latillas*. Bracket corbels are simply shaped and undecorated. A second-story balcony, small shuttered window and bed molding are visible on the far wall. Bed molding was used in Colonial homes to help distribute the weight of the vigas and prevent the walls from cracking.

This ceiling was salvaged from a nineteenth-century church in Northern New Mexico. The date "April 18–4" is carved into the beams, and drawings of altar pieces are visible on the planks. The center design is carved into the beam to resemble corbels. This is one of the most unusual ceilings in the Southwest.

Exterior second-story portal with peeled aspen *latillas* and round vigas. The corbel in the center and the lintel are one piece. The balustrade is hand-carved with a rope design and supported by lathe-turned poles.

Painted aspen *latillas* form a herringbone pattern between square-hewn beams. The carved post balcony is supported by beams with step-carved ends.

116

Chip-carved square beams and bracket corbels form the ceiling of this balcony area. Aspen *latillas* are laid in a herringbone design to complete the pattern of this traditional ceiling.

A variety of split cedar ceilings with vigas on 2-foot to 2 1/2-foot centers. The ceiling in the center features hand-split cedar alternating with fallen aspen *latillas.* In the ceiling at bottom, cedar forms a herringbone pattern between the vigas. The patterns become an important part of traditional ceilings, and help to set the mood of interior spaces. Though green aspen is sometimes used, taking gray fallen wood from the mountains has less impact on the fragile ecology. The sight of golden aspen leaves shimmering against the clear blue sky is the highlight of a southwestern fall.

A shelf just below ceiling level provides a place for this collection of Pueblo pottery. These pieces date to the early 1900s. They are painted with a variety of naturalistic and geometric patterns. The ceiling is split cedar set in a herringbone pattern between square-cut pine beams.

In the desert areas of Arizona and Northern Mexico native materials such as ocotillo, carrizo and the woody skeletons of giant cactus are often used as *latillas*. In this ceiling, saguaro is set in a herringbone pattern between pine viga logs. Dance masks from throughout North and South America decorate the walls.

Round stripped vigas form a sunburst design in this living room. Pine boards, or *tablas,* are laid above the vigas to form the ceiling.

Many southwestern homes utilized ceilings as a central part of their decor. This hallway has a portion of a fine collection of early American Indian baskets adorning the vigas and walls.

Alexander Girard designed this ceiling with skylight and mirror *nicho.* The vigas have been plastered to include their rounded shape in the cove.

This adobe dome under construction is an example of pure Moorish technique. Builders from Egypt assisted in the design and construction of this mosque near Abiquiu, New Mexico. Small adobe bricks are used to achieve the dome shape and are laid with the help of a guide string from a central pole. When finished, the ceiling will be plastered and painted white.

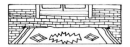

Floors

From the earliest pit-house structures until the arrival of milled lumber in the Southwest, the two basic choices for floors were earth or stone. Earth was most readily available and so was most widely used. The dirt was screened and dampened, then tamped to form the floor. Early Indian people used smooth floor-polishing stones to finish the surface, similar to the way traditional potters use a special stone to polish pottery. Later, a variety of binders such as milk, ox blood and even glue were used as hardeners for earth floors.

Though there are forests in the area, tools to cut wood were crude until the mid-1800s, so that wood was used only where there was no other substitute, and in mission churches. In 1840, it was reported that no more than six structures in the entire territory of New Mexico had wood floors. When the forts built lumber mills in the 1850s, the technology became widely available to saw lumber into boards, and wood floors became more common. Today, one rarely finds earth floors; they are fragile, temperamental and require constant care. Instead, most floors in traditional southwestern homes are flagstone, wood, Mexican tile, or brick laid in fanciful patterns.

Typical eighteenth-century room with a treadle loom for weaving rugs, blankets and *jergas* (floor coverings such as those in the foreground). The floor is brick, added after brick mills were established in the 1850s.

Opposite, top row. Brick standard paving run set in sand. 3-inch cedar rounds set in cement. Brick basket-weave pattern. *Second row.* Redwood 2 x 4 inches with stamped and painted cement. Mitered redwood cross filled with bricks. Brick floor. Pine plank floor with dowels. *Third row.* Mexican-style tile of Moorish design, dark grout. Mexican tile. Star design of river stones set in cement. *Bottom row.* Brick herringbone pattern. Flagstone. Zuni fetish design stamped in cement and painted. Redwood frame.

An example of an earth floor in the Martinez Hacienda in Taos, now part of the Kit Carson Foundation. Don Severino Martin (later Martinez) was active in the trade on the Chihuahua Trail; he owned caravans of *carretas* (carts) and pack mules. In this room are articles that were popular in the trade—bear hides, deer hides, saddles and other manufactured items.

Flagstone was the only alternative to earth floors until the late 1800s; this fine example is in the Minge home, a typical traditional adobe. The flagstone, found nearby, was laid in sand with small stones placed in a mosaic between the larger expanses.

Concrete stamped in a decorative pattern is often used in patio areas. This example is from Taos.

Jean and Oliver Seth's home in Santa Fe, with a highly glazed Mexican tile floor with dark grout. Tile, imported from Mexico, is a popular floor covering throughout the Southwest; its tan to reddish finish complements the adobe walls and Indian rugs so often found in traditional homes.

A wide plank floor of highly polished pine in a traditional pueblo-style home. Cut lumber was available after the establishment of mills in the 1850s and its use for flooring spread quickly.

This traditional Territorial adobe includes a pink and white Italian tile floor in the formal living room. A Rio Grande blanket from the 1890s is on the floor and an early Navajo transitional-period rug from about 1900 hangs on the wall.

Brick laid in a basketweave pattern in the Minge home. The *granero* dates from the 1800s and comes from the Rio Abajo area of New Mexico. Note the window shutter with pintle hinge set in a hand-adzed wood frame.

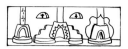

Fireplaces

For centuries the adobe fireplace has undergone change and modernization, but it has, in most cases, retained a certain basic aesthetic core epitomized in the "Indian-style" corner fireplaces of Taos Pueblo.

These high-arched, shallow and beautifully shaped corner fireplaces throw out a great deal of heat, and it is their line and grace that many builders attempt to copy today.

After the Pueblo Revolt of 1680–93, the Indians borrowed from the Spanish the structure of the fireplace, which replaced the firepit in the center of the room vented by a smoke hole in the ceiling. The first step toward a fireplace, according to Bainbridge Bunting in *Early Architecture in New Mexico*, was a corner hooded version much like the *fugoń de campaña*, a bell-shaped fireplace that developed from early hoods. From that version came the lovely corner structure, which often included a *padercita*, or stepped wall, which formed the corner.

The Territorial-style fireplace was not built extensively until after the Civil War with the increase of trade along the Santa Fe Trail and the coming of the railroad. This formal fireplace, close to Greek Revival style, retained the same shallow, reflective firepit, but became trimmed with Territorial wood molding. A mantel shelf was created and its location generally shifted from a corner to a flat wall.

We have today lost some familiarity with the simplicity, both structurally and aesthetically, of the Indian-style fireplace due to the construction of bulky, unattractive, elephantine shapes with inefficiently deep and nonreflective firepits.

It is due to the alarming continuance of this problem that we have chosen to show mostly examples of delicate and nonoverwhelming shapes. Also, we wish to share a few of the under-the-plaster construction details, which contribute to heat efficiency and to beauty of shape and line.

The fireplace need not be relegated to the living room alone, but is an attractive and warm addition to kitchen, bedroom, bath and portal. The appearance of the fireplace can be modified by the addition of *bancos* and kindling storage areas, or by a creative plaster job incorporating designs in relief and *nichos* and shapes incised with the hatchet or chisel, or (as the early Spanish did) by stenciling and painting the fireplace with natural earth colors.

Opposite, top. High bedroom fireplace with wood storage in hearth, 46 x 30 inches. Shepherd's bed fireplace, 2 1/2 x 9 feet. *Banco* by firepit, Rio Grande blanket on bed, chip-carved detailing on lintel. Typical corner fireplace against stepped half wall. *Middle.* Traditional fireplace with sculpted shallow *nichos* and incised design for damper handle. Hanging fireplace in dining area, window designed by Kristina Wilson. Oak-faced Territorial fireplace, 49 x 40 inches. Spanish Colonial retablos, santos, crosses, a Santa Clara pot, Taos drum and Navajo rug. *Bottom.* Mexican hanging fireplace with plaster hood and hearth painted with stencil designs. Red earth plaster on wainscot and arch surround. Corner fireplace on portal.

TRADITIONAL TAOS PUEBLO CORNER FIREPLACE
Building Sequence

I owe this knowledge to Marina Mirabel of Taos Pueblo, whose grandmother taught her in the traditional way passed on for generations. She showed Kristina Wilson the old way to build a fireplace, and Kristina taught me. Because the construction is unique, the results efficient, and the beauty of the shape unsurpassed, I want to share that knowledge.

From pit-house firepits of before 500 A.D. to the adobe fireplaces introduced by the Spanish in the 1600s, most homes did not have many (if any) windows other than a roof hole, and had one small doorway and a roof with at least a foot of dirt above it. Contemporary Taos Pueblo homes with windows and insulated roofs still consider the fireplace an important heat source.

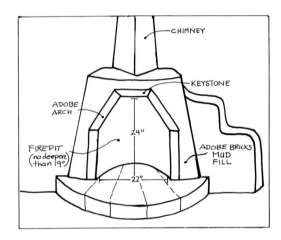

Most early Indians built fireplaces near the center of the living area against a specially constructed stepped wall. This placement warmed more area and increased the speed at which the warmth reached the room; an inside adobe wall heats up more rapidly than a colder exterior wall, and retains heat for a longer period of time. Once an adobe mass is warm, it takes very little additional heat to keep it so. An adobe fireplace will stay warm all night; even if it is not until late afternoon that another fire is built, the mass will quickly emanate heat. The Pueblo people did not let a room become cold as it would require a week's supply of wood to warm the walls again.

Before the introduction of cement (ca. 1880), fireplaces were built either on hard ground, stone slabs or large river rocks. Today a hole is dug about twelve inches deep and filled a few inches above ground level with cement and rocks to form the foundation.

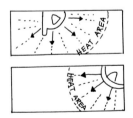

Step 1: The hearth is laid by shaping nonstabilized adobes, 4 x 8 x 12 inches, (mud mortar and mud plaster adhere better to regular adobes) with an old hatchet, and laying them in mud mortar. Spaces between adobes are filled with mud and adobe pieces. Pueblo women builders usually make their hearths no more than one adobe high, so that heat originates at the lowest possible point and rises and diffuses to warm more of the floor area.

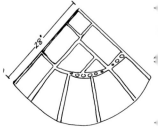

Step 2: The first two adobes for the firepit are selected. Use five adobes for the arch that are the most uniform and are without cracks or stones. Firepit adobes need to be shaped very slightly; chop the inner edge facing the wall at a *slight* angle to facilitate smooth plastering of the back of the firepit. The adobes are set upright in about 1/2 inch of mud ("sticky mud," with no sand or straw). They should be not quite parallel to the walls, with back edges touching the wall and front edges approximately 4 inches away from the wall. (See photos, modern construction.)

The shape of the firepit is critical to the performance of the fireplace. It must be slightly more open than a parabola in order to reflect heat out into the room. Most modern fireplaces, even those of this style, are built so that the heat reflects back and forth within the firepit, and does not extend more than a few feet into the room. An ideally built, true Indian-style fireplace should generate heat *at least* ten feet into the room.

The depth of the fireplace is another major factor in heat output. The Pueblo people rarely make a firepit deeper than 19 inches; most measure less than 16 inches. Logs are burned upright (tepee style) and according to a 1954 Forest Service study, wood burns more thoroughly and efficently when laid this way.

Step 3: The second set of adobes for the arch are shaped by angling the ends, chopping more off the top end. Some Taos Pueblo women do not change the bottom end at all, but rather wedge adobe chips and mud where the two uprights meet.

Step 4: The most important adobe, the keystone, is made at this time. It often has to be shaped several times as the first attempts with the hatchet might take off too much, get the angle wrong, or weaken the adobe. The sides of the keystone are angled to meet the uprights as nearly as possible, and the front side (towards the room) is always wider than the back by about three inches (depending on the placement of the first two uprights). (Please refer to the modern construction building sequence.)

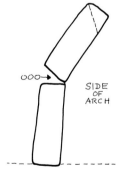

SIDE OF ARCH

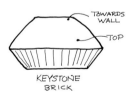

TOWARDS WALL

TOP

KEYSTONE BRICK

Step 5: Construction of the arch is tricky. Sticky mud and adobe chips for wedging should be ready at hand. Mud left overnight is often preferred: somehow it is stickier. Mud mortar 1/2 inch thick is placed on top of the two adobes already in place, and on the sides of the keystone before it is positioned. One upright can be held steady by a knee while the other is steadied with one hand. The keystone is then picked up with the other hand and placed in position. Often, the arch is propped up from underneath with boards until it sets. If the arch is not symmetrical, some adjustment can be made by maneuvering the arch while holding both sides. (Please refer to the modern construction building sequence.)

CORRECT

INCORRECT

This is basically a casual process, not one in which any other measurements than the depth of the firepit, height of the arch, and size of the throat where the chimney connects are important. Marina, who has built so many, never measures anything; she works from an instinctual easiness with the material, dabbing mud and adobe pieces here and there (particularly up inside the throat of the firepit) with both aesthetics and functionality in mind. If you are copying this process, it is important to suspend disbelief at several points. The arch skeleton is clumsy and awkward looking, but the next day you can stand right on top of it.

Step 6: Mud is immediately pressed gently into the joints of the arch, and smoothed over the entire arch to stabilize the structure.

Step 7: The space between the arch and the wall is filled with adobe pieces and mud. A flat plane is traditional here (rather than the rounded shape typical of the misnomered, recently created "kiva" style). This space is filled in to 4 inches below the top of the arch; each side is constructed with the shape of the firepit and the size of the chimney in mind.

Inside the firepit, about one quarter of the way up the second upright, the sides need gradually to narrow to meet the chimney opening (an opening approximately 8 1/2 x 8 1/2 inches). This is accomplished by shaping adobes for the sides that gradually "step" inwards, resulting in the ideal interior shape, something like a Coke bottle inside, and equally as smooth. The interior shape is critical to the performance of the fireplace; smoke must be allowed to flow smoothly. Pockets or indentations, especially in the throat area, will impede the flow, and force smoke to curl out into the room. If the areas are deeper than 3/4 inch to 1 inch, Marina packs mud and adobe chips in a gradual buildup.

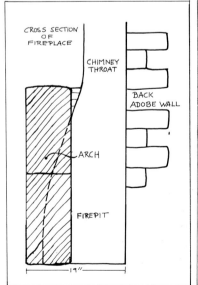

CROSS SECTION OF FIREPLACE

CHIMNEY THROAT

BACK ADOBE WALL

ARCH

FIREPIT

19"

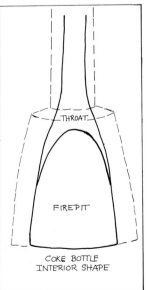

THROAT

FIREPIT

COKE BOTTLE INTERIOR SHAPE

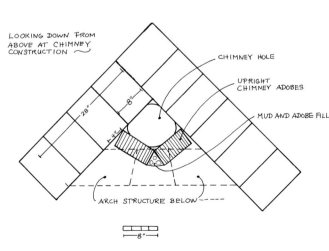

LOOKING DOWN FROM ABOVE AT CHIMNEY CONSTRUCTION

CHIMNEY HOLE

UPRIGHT CHIMNEY ADOBES

MUD AND ADOBE FILL

28"

8"

ARCH STRUCTURE BELOW

8"

Step 8: A hand-troweled coat of mud plaster (4 parts mud to 1 to 1 1/2 parts straw) is applied 1/4 to 1/2 inch thick. The plastered firepit is left to "set up" for a day before the chimney is begun. The sharp back corner is plastered to achieve a smooth arc.

Step 9: The chimney is comprised of mud-mortared adobe bricks, laid upright, and smoothly plastered inside as each course goes up. The chimney extends through the ceiling and about two feet above the firewall and the highest point on the roof. The hole cut in the roof is approximately 12 inches square to allow the adobes through. The interior smoke space is close to 8 inches round. Traditional fireplaces have no smoke shelf or damper.

Step 10: After a rough coat of plaster, again about 1/2 inch thick, the chimney is allowed to dry for a few days before the final plastering is started. A finish plaster of clay, finely chopped straw, and very little sand is mixed. (It is thought that too much sand reduces stickiness and weakens the surface, resulting in flaking of large chunks of plaster and chipping damage from logs and kindling.) If necessary, the firepit is reshaped with a hatchet to form the smooth Coke bottle shape. The surface is sprinkled with water so that the new plaster will adhere. Finish plaster is applied with pressure by the hands; a circular hand motion smooths it. When the plaster is partially dry, it is polished and smoothed again. If cracks appear, a thin wash of mud is worked onto the surface with an old piece of burlap or a sponge. This rubbing process also hardens the finish. Careful attention is paid to the interior surface as it is subject to much use and potential damage. Plaster is never applied over 3/4 inch thick, because it has a tendency to chunk off when dry, especially when plaster is applied to small areas. Plaster dries in a sheetlike unit and, if the surface is wet enough, it will bond quite well.

Step 11: The next focus is the final appearance, the line and shape of the whole fireplace. Plaster and finish work can entirely change the final form. If an aesthetic change is needed, mud is applied in layers, or adobe pieces and mud are added for more major changes. The shape can also be altered with a hatchet. The flexibility of the material allows for tremendous sculptural possibilities.

Step 12: Once the final plaster, rubbed free of cracks, is dry, a color slip of finely screened, soupy mud is wiped on the moistened surface with a piece of sheepskin or a sponge. Often, a darker earth color is chosen for the hearth and around the arch (areas more subject to damage and soot), and a lighter earth color is selected for the rest (usually the same color as the walls).
   The finished fireplace must be allowed to dry slowly and evenly. If a fire is built too soon, the intense heat in the firepit dries the plaster surface and the whole structure too quickly and unevenly, resulting in weak areas. After about a week a fireplace of unsurpassed beauty and long durability is ready for daily use—a permanent focal point of a home.

Temporary placement of adobes and firebrick to determine the open parabola shape.

Four courses of firebrick in place, the back straight, and the sides beginning to angle *slightly*.

Placement of next two uprights and keystone simultaneously.

Stabilization of the arch with mud. Note that the area between the first upright adobes and the wall on each side is filled with adobes and mud.

Skeleton after plaster stabilization. The sides between the arch and the wall will be completed along with the firebrick in the back to form the Coke bottle interior.

After placement of the flue tile, plastering and shaping inside the throat is done to achieve smooth smoke flow.

Damper is checked for ease of movement. Note upright adobe bricks in place to line flue tile through ceiling.

The completed fireplace.

A MODERN ADAPTATION OF THE TAOS PUEBLO TRADITIONAL
FIREPLACE
Building Sequence

The efficiency of the corner fireplace has been largely underestimated. The remarkable performance of this traditional fireplace is a result of the shape and depth of the firepit, the height of the hearth, the heat sink qualities of the adobe material used, the central location in a room, and the upright burn of the wood. Other contemporary fireplaces do not employ these time-proven guidelines (especially the reflective shape and shallowness of the firepit) and send far less heat into the room.

The aesthetics of the traditional style are unsurpassed in simplicity and elegance of line and shape. Many contemporary fireplaces, especially those built in "elephantine" style, are immense, and appear to have been built as a miniature mission church stage set. Others look as though the builder poured dough through the chimney hole and then poked a finger into the puddle at the bottom. These examples are extreme, but unfortunately common. Overbuilding and insensitivity to line have been the major aesthetic crimes; lack of attention to heat reflection is the major functional crime.

Materials Needed

50 to 60 nonstabilized adobes, 4 x 8 x 12 inches
2 lengths of 1/2-inch-square rod, approximately 14 inches long.
20 to 25 firebricks
2 pounds fire clay, or 1 gallon 'Sairset, a premixed, heat-resistant mortar from
  A. P. Green Refractories Co.
5 flue tiles 8 1/2 x 8 1/2 inches (depends on height of chimney, each flue
  tile 24 inches tall)
adobe dirt, finely chopped straw, plaster sand (or finer sand)
damper (see illustration)
4 to 5 four-inch strips of metal lath, 1/2 pound number 20 nails, about 25
  roofing nails, 1 1/2-inch size

Tools Needed

tinsnips, hammer, brick chisel, small cold chisel, old hatchet, small pointed trowel, wheelbarrow, shovel hoe, bucket, large brush, fine-mesh screen, tape measure

Before beginning to construct your fireplace, local, state and national building codes must be consulted and followed.

Step 1: The distance the firepit must be from any wood wall is usually specified (often 12 inches). In this example, the wall is entirely adobe. Chimney clearance is also an important specification. In New Mexico 6 inches is required. When flue tile is used, it must be covered on all sides with 4-inch adobe bricks. All wood is cut or chiseled away at least 6 inches. Many fires have started even after ten years because the flue tile was set next to a viga or roof boards.

Step 2: Each course of adobes (approximately 4 inches) for the hearth is laid with overlapping joints on a foundation of 18-inch cement and reinforced mesh (check codes for foundation specifics). The hearth in this example is high because the room is small, and the additional heat a lower hearth would provide at floor level is not a consideration here.

Step 3: If the corner chosen for the fireplace is a right angle, some shaping with the hatchet is necessary to achieve an open arc for the firepit and to maintain a traditional appearance. If firebrick is set directly into the corner the arc would be wrong. If firebrick is set out from the corner, maintaining the ideal arc, the entire structure would project too far into the room, and result both in an enormously fat chimney and very rounded sides (Figure A). Therefore, some of the corner must be chopped out; a few inches deep and 12 inches up usually does the trick (the sides of the arch and the firebricks begin to come out from the wall at that point). An adobe wall is a minimum of 12 inches thick, usually 14 to 16 inches, so this minor shaving is not a structural detriment (Figure B).

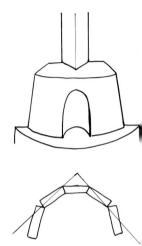

Step 4: Firebrick is cut to shape with a masonry blade on a circular saw (a wood form is made to hold the firebrick while sawing, and a dust mask should be worn while the saw is in operation), or with a brick chisel, striking a scored line.

Step 5: The first two adobes and first courses of firebrick are initially set in place without mortar to test the desired shape and depth of the firepit. Measurements at this time are important; a depth of not more than 19 inches and arch width at the lowest point of approximately 22 to 24 inches are desired. The arc of the fireplace must be quite open. (Please refer to both the construction photographs and the traditional Taos Pueblo building sequence throughout construction.)

Step 6: Firebrick must be mortared with heat-resistant clay (either fire clay or 'Sairset mortar). Construction or repair with cement does not work because cement pops, cracks and breaks down with heat. Between several courses of firebrick thin metal lath strips are placed to tie the firebrick to the adobe arch. These strips extend about 8 inches out from the firebrick on each side, and are nailed to the back of the first two upright adobes with roofing nails.

The firebrick in the back does not angle forward until it reaches a few inches *above* the top of the arch. If the back begins to slope sooner, the fireplace will smoke. The side firebricks arch slightly to match the adobe arch. The last courses of firebrick are added after the adobe construction is complete, and after the throat is gradually narrowed and brought up to flow smoothly into the flue tile in a Coke bottle shape.

Step 7: The fireplace structure should set up for a day before beginning the chimney. First, a flue tile, 8 1/2 x 8 1/2 inches, is prepared for the damper before it is secured in place. The damper is a made-to-order steel square with slightly rounded corners which fits just inside the flue tile (Figure C). A 1/2- to 3/4-inch-square steel rod with a handle welded to it (an old bit or key . . .) is welded to the steel plate. A V-shaped groove is chiseled into both sides of the first flue tile with a cold chisel to accommodate the damper rod. To test the damper's fit and movement within both tiles, the second flue tile is set on the first, with damper in place. If the groove is correct, the damper should stay solidly in either the open or closed position without spinning or shifting. Although the damper is rarely used in a partially open position, this option should be assured as well.

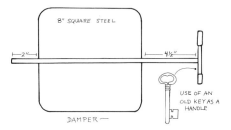

8" SQUARE STEEL

2"

4½"

USE OF AN OLD KEY AS A HANDLE

DAMPER

Step 8: To support the flue tiles on the structure, two lengths of 1/2-inch-square steel rod are necessary to disperse the weight of the chimney. Rods are cut approximately 14 inches long and are hammered 3 to 4 inches into the back wall. They rest on the firebrick in back and the arch in front. The flue tile is then placed on mud mortar and secured to the wall (also coated with mud) by a strip of metal lath. Mud is then plastered inside the chimney opening from underneath to assure a smooth smoke flow. The mud should be sticky (no sand but with some straw). Indentations or pockets in the Coke bottle shape cause the smoke to circle and sneak out.

Step 9: About 1/4 to 1/2 inch of 'Sairset mortar is troweled on the flue tile, but not on the damper or groove, and the second flue tile is set on top. The mortar that oozes out is smoothed inside and out. The damper should be checked again for ease of movement, and checked throughout the process in case mortar has spread onto the works.

Step 10: Adobes are set in mud in the upright position next to the slightly mudded flue tile, and continue up and out the chimney hole. On a flat roof, the chimney should rise about two feet higher than the highest point on the roof, fire walls included. On a pitched roof, the chimney must be higher than the highest point of the pitch, unless it is at least 8 to 10 feet away from that point. Due to wind draft patterns along the roof, a fireplace often smokes when the chimney isn't high enough.

The functional problems of bonding adobe to firebrick are solved with the use of metal lath, but nothing is as satisfactory as adobe on adobe. Areas that might flake in future years (especially in the throat of the fireplace, causing the smoke to curl out) are fairly easily repaired. First the soot must be wire-brushed clean, and the adobe well moistened before repairs can begin. Gradual layers of mud plaster (1/4 to 1/2 inch thick, allowing each layer to dry) are applied to the damaged areas.

In conclusion, the only aesthetic problems that arise from the use of modern materials can be fairly easily dealt with. The visible firebrick can be washed over with a thin slip of mud, which will adhere for years, or firebrick can be laid in pleasing patterns. A chimney made with flue tiles is fatter than the traditional model, but a builder with a good eye can, with plaster, bring the wall out to meet the chimney at a different point, thereby changing the line and appearance of a structure as well. *Nichos* and other incised designs can break up the space, making it appear smaller, and relief work can often make an area seem larger.

This Hopi Indian woman is making piki bread on a stone slab fireplace with a hooded opening in the roof. Piki bread, made from a thin gruel of cornmeal, is painted onto the hot stone by hand and cooks into paper-thin strips, which are folded and served on ceremonial occasions. *Photo ca. 1915, courtesy Museum of New Mexico, neg number 21596.*

Putting the finishing touches on the chimney, this Hispanic woman daubs mud on the bricks that were set on end to form the chimney opening. Note the unusual octagon-cut vigas in the ceiling. *Photo Jesse L. Nusbaum, ca. 1912, courtesy Museum of New Mexico, neg number 61635.*

This corner fireplace was constructed soon after Don Antonio Severino Martinez moved to Taos in 1804. Hide-covered saddle bags and a pack saddle sit on the adobe floor to the left.

Plaster designs form a scallop pattern on this heavy square-shaped corner fireplace at Rancho de las Golondrinas. A Mexican water canteen hangs on the chimney, and a Santo Domingo Pueblo water jar rests on the adobe floor.

Fireplace built in traditional Indian style at Taos Pueblo by Cruzita Mondragon in 1949. The stepped wall and mantel are decorated by pottery from Zia and Acoma pueblos; a black pottery wall sconce from Santa Clara Pueblo hangs from the chimney.

Spanish Colonial retablos surround this fireplace built by Annie Archuleta of Taos.

Classic corner fireplace built by Kristina Wilson in Taos. Symmetrical *nichos* on either side of the chimney hold Hopi kachinas and Zuni fetishes. Other decorations include beaded mocassins, a Hopi basket, an inlaid straw cross and iron tools.

141

Flat wall fireplace in a traditional pueblo-style home. The fireplace is the focal point of the room; huge logs are burned horizontally in the firepit.

A traditional corner fireplace plastered with *tierra bayita* (a tan earth); the damper handle is a bridle bit.

This unique corner fireplace of a more European design is in the Nicolai Fechin home in Taos.

Spanish-style fireplace built by Ward Alan Minge. Many early Spanish fireplaces had a wooden mantel lintel instead of an adobe arch.

Large pueblo-style corner fireplace. The structure sits farther out from the corner than more traditional examples.

This shepherd's bed in Santa Fe is part of the original de la Peña home built in 1845, which is now owned by Gerald and Katie Peters.

A flat wall fireplace in the living room in the Fechin home, Fechin Institute, Taos.

Tile-lined hearth and bedroom fireplace in the Robert and Janice Daigh home at Los Cordovas, New Mexico. The fireplace opening is indented as a visual motif. Note the colcha embroidery of San Ysidro, the patron saint of farmers and the village of Los Cordovas.

Two fireplaces in the home and studio of sculptor Juan Hamilton. The upper fireplace and chimney are built into the adobe wall, leaving only a simple opening. The lower fireplace, in the living room, is faced with stone and has a mantel the length of the wall.

Opposite, top left. Moorish-influenced corner fireplace with unusual keyhole-shaped opening and sculpted *banco* area. In a bedroom in Carefree, Arizona.

Opposite, top right. Counter-level kitchen fireplace designed and built by Sandy Seth. The foundation for the fireplace extends through the tiled counter to the floor.

Opposite, below left. This breakfast room fireplace, also in the Daigh home, sits above a wood storage area, and features a brick hearth and decorative tiles set around the fireplace opening.

Opposite, below right. A Zia reindeer bowl is inset into the plaster above the firepit of this flat-wall fireplace with step-walled mantel. In one of the original rooms of the Oscar Berninghaus home, now owned by Robert and Sandra Daughters.

Two fireplaces built back to back, designed by Mark and Art Adair in Taos. The larger fireplace is the main focus of the living room, the smaller faces the kitchen and dining area.

Opposite. The line and shape of this corner fireplace embody the traditional style. The painting "Amaryllis" is by Georgia O'Keeffe.

Unique early Territorial-style adobe fireplace with micaceous *tierra amarilla* plaster highlights. An *alacena,* or cabinet, is set into the mud plaster at left.

Charming kitchen fireplace in the home of Genevieve Janssen in Taos. The *alacena* at right was made at the Santa Fe Indian School in 1910.

Hanging fireplace with tile detailing, in Taos.

Unusual hanging fireplace in the dining room of the traditional pueblo-style home built by the late Taos artist Robert Ellis.

Corner fireplace in a Territorial home in Nambe. The arch opening and mantel are squared at the edges, and the hearth is triangular.

Traditional shepherd's-bed fireplace at Rancho de las Golondrinas. As well as being the kitchen stove, the shepherd's bed kept people warm while sleeping, and was used to dry herbs and other staples. A cradle of wood and leather hangs from the ceiling.

Mexican colonial fireplace in a home in the Catalina foothills of Tucson, Arizona.

A *fogón de campana* (Spanish for bell-shaped fireplace), which allowed a cook to work at both open sides. In the Kit Carson Museum in Taos, originally built in 1825.

Modern sculpted fireplace and *banco* area designed and built by Malcolm Brown, Taos, in the home of Judith Buck.

An ornate gilded mirror reflects a flat-walled fireplace with high open arch, in a historic house on Alameda Street in Santa Fe.

An example of a shallow, reflective firepit and a high open arch are seen in this fireplace. Wood is stacked on end to allow for thorough burning.

Carved and painted Indian corn motif mantel on a large adobe fireplace in Santa Fe. The corn is painted red, yellow and blue—sacred colors to the Indians, and the natural colors of native corn.

A variety of fireplaces adapted to outside areas. These fireplaces are plastered with cement stucco to protect them from the weather. Outdoor seating arrangements face each of the fireplaces. A high, hanging fireplace is pictured, with a Mexican wrought-iron lamp hanging above.

This formal Territorial fireplace with wooden columns and capitals in Nambe is a Spanish Colonial copy of a marble fireplace. At left is a carved and painted Cristo from Northern New Mexico with articulated limbs. It represents the tradition of carving that is part of the Penitente brotherhood and religion.

Classic Territorial corner fireplace with wooden facing trim and mantel, in the Rancho de Chimayo Restaurant in Chimayo, New Mexico.

Bill Tull of Phoenix designed this modern adobe fireplace with marble-faced opening. The firebrick is laid in a herringbone pattern in the firepit area.

154

The library of the Minge home near Albuquerque features this typical Territorial fireplace dating from about 1900. Early Territorial fireplaces were a folk adaptation of designs first introduced in the 1880s from eastern United States. A colcha of the Virgin of Guadalupe from the Governor Conway home in Peralta, New Mexico, hangs from a carved bed molding.

The *horno* is an Arabic-influenced Spanish introduction to the Southwest. It was used for baking, especially for bread, and is still in common use throughout the Indian pueblos, and in some rural Hispanic villages. Cleofas M. Jaramillo recalls, in *Shadows of the Past*, that, "On Monday and Tuesday of Holy Week the conical adobe ovens were seen smoking . . . while the week's supply of bread was being baked. The mud ovens must be blessed before using them, or they won't bake the bread right; it will come out soggy. To bless the oven, salt is sprinkled on the cross and prayers recited." Pictured are a row of three *hornos* built by Carmen Velarde in the Martinez Hacienda at Taos, and two single *hornos* from Santa Fe and Taos. On the facing page, an adobe arch echos the curves of this *horno* in Taos.

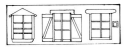

Windows and Shutters

Pre-Spanish dwellings had only small rooftop entrances and few (if any) windows. Windows were still rare in the seventeenth and eighteenth centuries when the newly introduced ground-level doors provided the only light and ventilation. Windows, when they did exist, were small, high on the wall, and on only one side of a room. In *placita* homes, for protective reasons, they faced the central courtyard. In linear houses, windows faced the east or south for light and heat. End windows were always rare. Early window openings were barred with wood gratings or heavy shutters for protection and insulation, and some windows were glazed with translucent minerals like mica or selenite. Oiled paper, cloth and rawhide also served as early glazings. Painted curtains or tissue paper cut into complex designs substituted for popular but expensive lace curtains.

In Arizona, where the Spanish Colonial art of elaborate plaster ornamentation flourished, windows are often decorated with carved plaster curtains, shell motifs and other designs of European origin.

When the railroad arrived in the 1880s, clear glass and prefabricated window sashes and frames became available, and were immediately popular. In Territorial adobes, windows and shutters are often trimmed with jigsaw-cut folk motifs in imitation of Victorian-style molding.

Modern window adaptations have had varying successes fitting into the feel and look of a traditional adobe home. Metal casings jar the eye and interfere with the soft adobe texture. Large picture windows can dominate a wall, yet many modern thermopane wood sash windows adapt well to traditional-style homes, as do skylights, a popular new variation of the ancient use of roof holes as a source of light.

Taos Pueblo North, ca. 1920. Note that most entries are on the second level. The windows are quite small and are either glazed with mica, unglazed, or spindled with wood. *Photo T. Harmon Parkhurst, courtesy Museum of New Mexico, neg number 12463.*

Opposite, top row. Three Territorial trimmed windows. Standard paned arch before the application of trim, each 2 1/2 x 2 feet. *Second row.* Scallop top trim. Three formalized territorial adaptations with cornice and dentil detailing. Scallop overlay with split and turned spindles, 2 1/2 x 1 1/2 feet. *Third row.* Plexiglass sandwiched in wood cross design, 1 1/2 feet x 1 1/2 inches. Double-glazed window with painted Penasco-design shutters. Reverse painting, 1 1/2 x 1 1/2 feet. *Fourth row.* Pediment variations from Northern New Mexico, jigsaw cut and carved. *Bottom row.* Two cross motif Penasco shuttered windows, 4 x 2 feet.

159

This window, now in the Minge home, was originally from the Governor Conway house in Peralta, New Mexico, and dates to ca. 1910. Its deep window-box frame and plain shutters are classic examples of Territorial style. An S-shaped hook holds the open shutters against the adobe wall.

Early folk adaptation of Territorial-style trim and applied ornamentation. Rancho de las Golondrinas.

Colonial-period window opening with wooden bars and pintle hinge shutters; the wall is over 2 feet thick. Martinez Hacienda, Taos.

Greek Revival style window with applied trim, and pediment built out from the adobe wall. Possibly the window was bought ready-made at the turn of the century to install in this traditional Territorial home in Nambe.

Simple wood trim decorated with *miligritos* from Mexico (small tin representations of animals or parts of the body that are pinned with prayers to the robes of carved saints in churches throughout Mexico).

Territorial-style pedimented window trim, ca. 1900. Window glass arrived in quantity by 1880 and was used in small muntined windows throughout the Territorial period.

Palladian-influenced arched window in the Ranchos de Taos Church, one of three pairs. A corresponding window can be seen on the far wall. Corbel ends are visible below the exposed vigas.

Sash window set into thick adobe wall of a pueblo-style home. The wrought iron is fashioned in a modern, art nouveau design. A carved Mexican figure and an Indian pot rest on the curved sill.

In the village of El Fuerte, part of the Fort Lowell Historical Site. This window in the home remodeled by Edward and Ros Spicer is typical of the Arizona-Sonora style of the 1930s.

This decorative trim is painted on the window frames and wall in a colorful folk pattern of pears and leaves, in Taos.

Classic, undecorated Territorial four-pane window, set into a mud plaster wall at the Minge home north of Albuquerque. Agave and century plants grow in the porous soil.

Many-paned window set into deep adobe walls in the Mabel Dodge Luhan complex; though the building is in Pueblo style, the window elements are of Territorial derivation.

Interior of the Mabel Dodge Luhan home at Las Palomas Educational Retreat. Note the Territorial-style balustrade and deep-silled sash window painted Taos blue.

The home of Dr. and Mrs. Albert Simms in Santa Fe, built in Territorial style, overlooks a spectacular view of the Tesuque Valley.

Carved and painted Indian corn motif surrounding a window in Taos. Built in 1948, this is the last home built and occupied by Mabel Dodge Luhan, the famous art patron.

Floor to ceiling windows line this atrium wall in Nambe. This is a traditional solution to a bank of windows, and is more visually appealing than large panes of glass. Posts and corbels mark the entry. Note the mud plaster and high fire wall with drainage *canale*.

Many dormer windows were added to this pitched tin roof in the early 1930s. Ladders (which are locally called "chicken ladders") are often left attached to the roof for easy access for repairs.

This typical Territorial-style pitched roof adobe in Northern New Mexico features two symmetrical dormer windows set into the second story to provide extra space and light.

Dormer windows highlight the second story of the L-shaped adobe home of the Martinez family in Truchas, New Mexico, a classic mountain-style Territorial home.

This domed skylight in Arizona painted in a Pueblo Indian pottery motif with soft desert colors adds an unusual and creative touch to the bath and dressing room area of this adobe home.

Sculptor Juan Hamilton's studio in Tesuque. Deep, single-paned floor to ceiling windows provide north light and a view of the surrounding countryside.

Unusual plaster mullioned window on the mosque in Abiquiu, New Mexico.

Plaster curtains, Spanish-style coat-of-arms and a sill from San Miguel in plaster relief surround this small entry window in Tucson.

Plaster shell motif over the entrance door to Tumacacori National Monument in Arizona. Tumacacori was one of the earliest Jesuit Mission churches; it was established by 1700, abandoned, reconstructed and abandoned again. Many of the architectural elements were Moorish in origin.

Beautifully arched corner fireplace in the Minge home. Proportioned for its function as heat disperser, the traditional corner fireplace is also an important aesthetic feature of southwestern homes. Note the decorative *senefa,* or stencil, of bird designs.

The Fechin home in Taos. A European influence is evident in the wood
detailing, window treatment and the massive central fireplace.

Annie Archuleta of Taos built this fireplace on the portal of Edwin Bewley's home. She was responsible for maintaining many of the old traditions of building, and passed them on to interested apprentices in the Taos valley.

This colorful fireplace is brightly painted with Mexican designs and other folk motifs. The side paneling continues around the room, a dining area in the popular Rancho de los Caballeros in Wickenburg, Arizona, an adobe dude ranch built in the 1940s.

Pink petunias flourish in this north-facing window box near Taos. The Territorial window frame is painted Taos blue, a color that is believed to ward off evil spirits.

Blue Gate pastel, 12 x 14 inches, by Valerie Graves.

Spring blossoms. Pastel 12-1/4 x 19 inches, by Valerie Graves.

A unique portal in Nambe, New Mexico, painted with fanciful folk animals, flowers and angels.

Simple wooden gates lead from a Taos portal into the large living room of this adobe home. The spindles in the top sixth of the doors create interesting patterns as well as letting in light and air. The vessel at right is from Mexico, as is the straw stand it rests upon.

Edwin Bewley's Taos portal; the colors are muted echos of the colors surrounding this traditional home—the blue of the sky, the red-tinted earth and the tan
clays and hills.

Unassuming door with flat spindles in a Santa Fe patio. The bronze sculpture
is by Juan Hamilton.

The dome over the nave of the San Xavier Mission, elaborately painted with two rosette windows. The plaster rosette design is a typical signature of Spanish-style buildings. At center is a representation of the Good Shepherd.

Designed by John Gaw Meem, these shutters close over a 6-foot window in the living room of Jean and Oliver Seth's home in Santa Fe. The shutters are built to open in the center in pairs of two. The carved and spindled wooden base doubles as a radiator cover.

Carved plaster shell *nicho* in the Tumacacori Mission near Tucson.

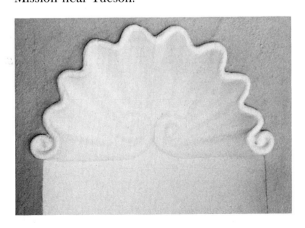

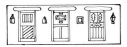

Doors and Doorways

The earliest doorways were small roof hatches or side doorholes covered with reed mats, skins, blankets or flat stones. For many years, doors remained small for defense, and to keep out the extremes of weather. The sills were raised to keep water from running into the rooms, and the lintels were low to keep heat in the room.

Wooden doors were first introduced by the Spanish for use in mission churches and some larger homes. A wooden door was a recognized symbol of prestige. A great deal of energy and scarce material was needed to make a door, something only the clergy and the wealthy could afford. Lt. George Gibson, who was stationed in Santa Fe in 1846, described a doorway in the Palace of the Governors that was covered with tanned cowhide painted to resemble wood in an effort to keep up appearances.

Most eighteenth-century wooden doors were simply decorated hand-hewn panels, hinged by a carved wooden peglike extention that fit into the doorframe. These are called pintle hinges, and the doors are called puncheon or, in the Southwest, *zambullo* doors. The puncheon door has been traced to the Near East as far back as 4000 B.C. From there, the door design spread to Europe, Africa, and, via Arab traders, to Spain.

The more standard battened door began to replace the *zambullo* by the mid-nineteenth century, after hand tools, iron nails and hinges were more easily available. The railroad brought ready-made doors, moldings and the pediments that became the hallmark of Territorial-style buildings. Often, hand-planed molding was nailed onto milled lumber boards in a two-ply pattern, which evolved into folk-style doors made in the Northern New Mexican villages of Truchas, Los Luceros, Rodarte, Llano, Chacon and Penasco in the nineteenth century. Now called Penasco doors, they are composed of hand-made moldings and fanciful jigsaw designs of crosses, stars, diamonds and other geometrical patterns.

This Spanish Colonial mission church door, now in the Millicent Rogers Museum in Taos, dates to the early 1800s and is deeply carved on alternating vertical and horizontal panels.

Opposite, top. Pine door with overlay of cross design cut from panels 1 x 8 inches. Cross design molding with square panels incised and painted with flowers. Contemporary Penasco-style door. Traditional Penasco-style door with jigsaw-cut designs. *Middle.* Traditional design elements, recess areas painted blue. Triple cross created by molding and raised panels. Diamond-cut pieces forming stars glued and nailed to pine door. Classic Penasco door, the lower half with molding strips on the diagonal. *Bottom.* Contemporary cross and flower designs jigsaw cut and applied to door. Cross variation with traditional cutout designs. Double crosses created by raised panels and applied molding. Flower motif carved in low relief on center panel.

179

This pintle hinge door in the Minge home is an excellent example of the earliest Colonial-style door openings. Note the raised sill, stone threshold and small size, 5 x 3 feet. The wall is the width of the door—over 3 feet!

A simple floral design relief carved in a single plank metal-hinged door at Las Palomas in Taos.

An illustration of the prestige associated with wooden doors; this huge door is a *trompe l'oeil* wall painting in the San Xavier Mission.

An early example, ca. 1870, of a carved door from Mexico with flower pot and floral arrangement in light relief. Note the escutcheon lock and raised sill.

Double Spanish Colonial doors with carved panels. The top panel opens inward. A carved stone decorative lintel is set in the plaster above the doorway.

Rosette windows, flower pots and cherubs adorn this carved Mexican door, made recently in the style of earlier designs.

Designed and hand-carved by Elidio Gonzales of Taos, this arched door and doorway features many Spanish design elements, including rosettes, conchas and rope braid. The small arch at center opens inward in colonial style.

Simply decorated Territorial-style doors. The doorframe is chip-carved to appear hand-adzed.

Elaborately carved door frame and door. The designs include corn and harvest motifs painted in light washes of color.

Below, left. Carved entry doors in the style of early mission doors. Both doors and window are set into deep recesses in the adobe wall.

Swinging double door carved in high relief by Nicolai Fechin, a Russian artist who moved to Taos in 1927. The design elements are a unique combination of Russian, Spanish and Moorish influences.

The front doors of the San Francisco de Assisi Mission church in Ranchos de Taos, a classic example of folk style adaptations of Gothic Revival designs.

Territorial doors installed in the Palace of the Governors in Santa Fe. Though the original building was constructed in 1610, milled lumber for Territorial-style doors was not available until the establishment of Fort Marcy in 1851.

Example of a typical, milled lumber Territorial-style door, set into a plain wooden frame, also of milled lumber. Doors such as these began to appear by 1890.

Modern folk variation: This ready-made door has been painted with various santo designs, including St. Francis, Santiago, San Ysidro and San Pascual.

José Dolores Lopez from Cordova, New Mexico, carved this screen door in the 1920s. Mr. Lopez's imaginative designs were especially popular in Santa Fe, though today few examples of his work survive.

Classic Territorial entryway and door. Each element—the pedimented doorway and door frame with arched windows, the applied decoration, and the carved balustrade—reflects its Queen Anne style origins.

Double Territorial doors with Queen Anne style transom windows, set into a soft plastered adobe wall. Glass windows, ready-made doors and the oil paint to finish them all arrived by railroad after 1880.

Large panes of glass are set into the double arches of this Territorial door with applied framework and spindled screens. This is the doorway to the patio of the Minge home north of Albuquerque.

The mountain villages of Northern New Mexico developed a unique folk-style door popularly called Penasco style (after one of these villages). This door with cutout arch and geometrical designs is a typical early example. A lace curtain hangs inside the windows.

Classic Penasco-style door.

Three examples of Penasco-style doors, depicting the innovative uses of decorative molding and raised and recessed panels. Often these doors are painted with Taos blue highlights, or with a wash of red earth paint. The cross designs were first used in chapel doors, but are now common in many homes in Northern New Mexico. Other designs include stars, squares and many geometric variations.

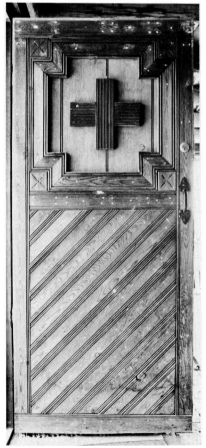

Penasco-style door from the 1930s of hand-sawn lumber and handmade molding applied to a base of pine planks.

A wide arch in the Paul and Jan Johnson home in Taos serves as the entryway to the kitchen and dining area with corner fireplace, tile floors and skylights.

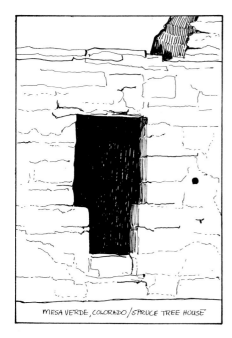

MESA VERDE, COLORADO / SPRUCE TREE HOUSE

Drawing of a classic T-shaped doorway. The reason for this shape is a mystery; these doorways occur at kiva entrances and plaza entryways. One of the theories is that the shape evolved to accommodate large headdresses on dancers and other ceremonial participants.

Tufa cliffs in the Pajarito Plateau area near Los Alamos, New Mexico, provided shelter for the early inhabitants of this area. These caves were occupied from about 1400 to 1500 by the Anasazi Indians who also built extensive mud and stone pueblos. Tufa, a hardened volcanic ash, is quite soft; these entryways were carved from the rock. *Photo ca. 1925, Courtesy Museum of New Mexico, neg. number 131790.*

A passageway between the two *placitas* at the Martinez Hacienda in Taos connected the two protected areas of this eighteenth-century structure.

This pointed arch at Las Palomas is of an unusual shape. Through the doorway is a traditional corner fireplace by Anita Rodriguez of Taos.

191

Carved stone entryway in Tucson, originally from a church in San Juan del Reyes, Mexico, built in 1693. The wooden entry doors are also hand-carved and come from Guanajuato, Mexico. A portion of a stone mosaic floor of the sun, moon and stars is visible through the open door.

Below, left. A high crenellated wall forms the dramatic entryway to the worshiping area of the mosque in Abiquiu. The door and doorway are arched and deeply recessed.

Arches within arches in the adobe mosque at Abiquiu, New Mexico. The vaulted adobe ceiling is Moorish in design.

The entryway to the living room of Elaine and Arnold Horwitch's Santa Fe home. This deep, sculpted arch shape with a pine lintel gives the space a sense of solidity and openness.

Cabinets

In the Southwest, the first cabinets were probably basketry storage jars fashioned by early inhabitants called, appropriately, "Basket Makers." These jars were portable and so could be carried on hunting and gathering migrations, or utilized to gather water and to irrigate fields. Later, exquisite pottery was made throughout the Southwest and decorated in a dazzling array of patterns and designs. These pots were often buried under floors or stored along trails for emergency rations of food and water.

Small holes cut into the sandstone cliff walls or shaped into the adobe walls were also used for stashes of food or ceremonial items. In adobe homes today, these are still common decorative accents, called *nichos.*

The Spanish built wooden cabinets into the wall. These are called *alacenas,* a word that comes from the Arabic *aljizena,* which means a small basket, a hole in the wall for storage, or a cupboard. The first *alacenas* in the Southwest were simple and, until metal was more available, had wooden pintle-hinged doors. They were often decorated with carvings and painted with earth pigments. Nineteenth- and twentieth-century cabinets include tall spindled chests called *trasteros* (*trastos* is Spanish for china, kitchen utensils, etc.) and tin-fronted cupboards. The tin was punched with small holes in a rosette design to allow for the circulation of air (and keep out flies). Leather trunks, carved chests and large *graneros* (grain holders) are also common. Today's homes contain modern adaptations of these forms; even televisions, stereos and refrigerators are disguised by *trasteros.*

Alacena with double doors and pintle hinges; the design elements are divided into thirds in this unusual early example of a built-in cabinet.

Opposite, top. Three classic Northern New Mexican *alacenas.* The center one features a tin punched door. All approximately 22 x 26 inches. *Middle.* Dovetail chest, copy of a seventeenth-century Spanish Colonial design, 20 feet x 41 inches. Cedar-lined footed chest painted and carved, ca. 1958, 19 x 40 inches. *Bottom. Trastero* with raised and incised flower motif panels from Mexico, 76 1/2 x 36 inches. Small *trastero* with deep rosette relief, 54 x 18 inches. Cabinet with Penasco-style cross application, 77 x 36 inches.

This *alacena* in the kitchen of Genevieve Janssen in Taos was made in Penasco in 1910.

Made in shop class in the Taos High School, this small *alacena* serves as a spice cabinet, hanging conveniently next to the stove.

Lightning-pattern spindles decorate this Colonial-period *alacena* with pintle hinges. The metal pull was added after iron was more readily available.

196

Open doors reveal the scallop-carved shelves in this all-spindle *alacena* set in a slight recess in the adobe wall.

Earth colors in a light wash of blue and buff highlight the carved and spindled decorations of this classic and elegant *alacena*.

This handsome wardrobe is European in style and form, with wide doors and undecorated top. The date 1660 is carved in the right door in a fine script.

Classic Territorial-style wardrobe made from milled lumber, about 1890. The Gothic Revival base is similar to designs seen on folk-style doors in Northern New Mexico.

Mexican *trastero* with arched door carved in deep relief.

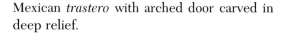

Trasteros are standing cabinets, usually with double doors. This fine eighteenth-century example shows the tall, narrow proportion and a typical scalloped top edge.

To meet modern times, this *trastero*, built in traditional style, disguises the stereo, television and tape player. Carved in the popular motifs carried on through time—Spanish lions, rosettes and rope-carved spindles.

One wall of the living room/dining area of this Taos home features a large (7 x 12 feet) built-in storage area modeled after traditional *trasteros*. Designed and built by Sandy Seth.

Helen Cordero, a Cochiti Pueblo potter famous for her "storyteller" ceramics, made the figures now at home in this early Spanish Colonial style *trastero*.

Two angels painted in Spanish Colonial style hang over a *granero* on this portal in Nambe. Peacock feathers from birds on the farm sit in a vase on the chest.

An ancient cottonwood log fashioned into a *granero* at Rancho de Las Golondrinas. The small opening cut into the top can be closed with a piece of wood or a stone.

Small painted chest with scallop and spindle design stand dating to about 1910. A New Mexican folk adaptation of Spanish Colonial designs.

Top, right. Plain Mexican pine chest made from hand-cut wood, about 1870. A *jerga* of wool can be seen covering a flagstone floor. Also note the tin candle sconces and colcha embroidery, all very typical of the late nineteenth century in New Mexico.

Carved Spanish Colonial chest with lion motif blends with the African carvings around it. (A grainery door from the Dogon tribe, with guardian human figures, stands at left.)

Traveling chest with separate stand. Note the dovetail joints, pegged stand and leather hinge. From the Martinez Hacienda in Taos.

Spindles

Spindles are both decorative and protective. The first spindles were simple wooden saplings, either stripped of their bark or left plain. Today, spindles are carved, painted and decorated in many creative ways. On a cabinet, spindles help to protect the contents; in a window spindles serve to keep people, birds and animals from entering. On any surface, spindles provide texture, pattern and distinctive decoration.

Garden gate with lathed spindles set in alternating fashion to create an interesting pattern of positive and negative spaces.

Opposite, top row. Balcony of unpainted turned spindles supported by chip-carved corbels. *Second row.* Grille of jigsaw-cut spindle, Southern Colorado. *Third row.* Variety of turned jigsaw-cut and hand-carved spindles from throughout the Southwest. *Fourth row.* Three *rejas* (grilles). *Bottom row.* Penasco-style balusters on a Territorial-style balcony; note the positive and negative spaces.

Tierra amarilla plaster frames this window opening with turned spindles. Small horizontal windows such as this were common in early homes of the nineteenth century.

These spindles were custom lathed so that the knotted rope design would form an arch when set into this garden gate. A scalloped metal piece protects the wooden gate frame.

Carved and painted second-story balcony of the Fine Arts Museum in Santa Fe.

Three different spindle designs are combined to form these chapel railings and priest's chair. The chair is almost Shaker in design, a contrast to the carved and drilled spindles that form the movable railings.

205

Copper tubing forms the spindles of this door and transom in a home near Phoenix.

Spindles designed by John Gaw Meem, on the Presbyterian Church in Santa Fe, also built by Meem. Meem was famous for respecting and reviving traditional adobe architecture. His attention even turned to small details, as evidenced in this unique window treatment.

Opposite. View from the second-story balcony that was added to the traditional de la Peña home in 1917. A rope-carved banister is in the foreground.

Simple turned spindles in an inset window at San Xavier Mission near Tucson. The plaster curve below is part of the elaborately carved facade of the church.

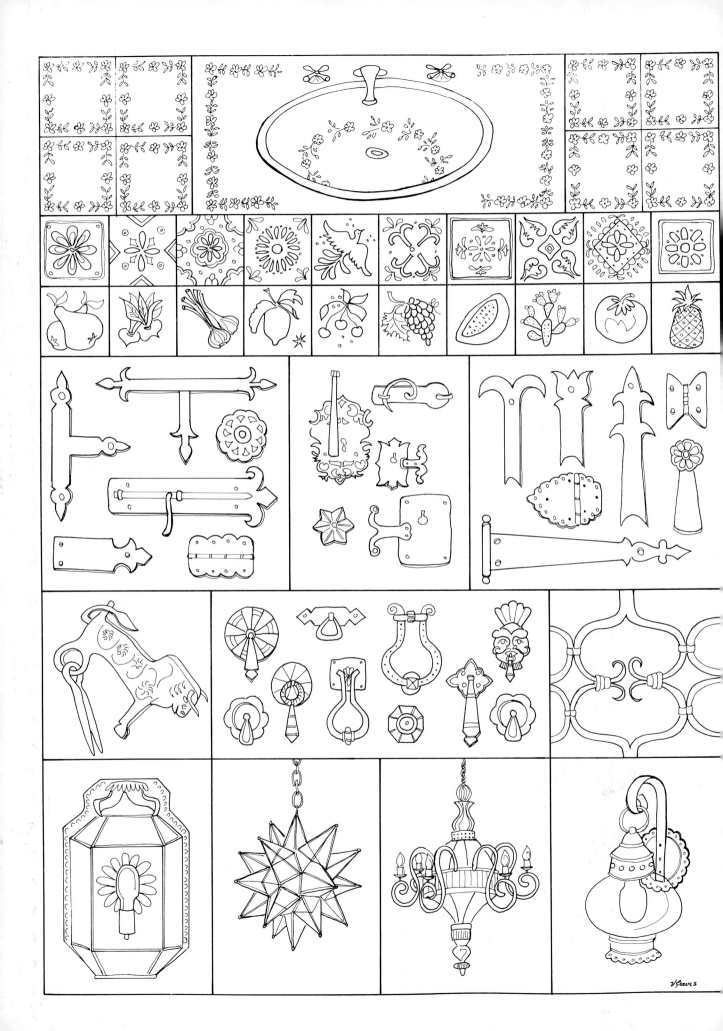

Tile, Hardware and Lighting

Tile was not commonly used in the Southwest (especially New Mexico) until late in the nineteenth century. In California and Texas the Spanish began ceramic production soon after their arrival, and manufactured roof tiles and fired bricks, but floor tiles and decorative tiles for kitchens and baths were not introduced until well into the twentieth century. Hand-painted Mexican tiles rapidly became popular in Traditional Pueblo and Arizona-Sonora style adobes as floor surfaces and for many other decorative applications.

Hardware was a rare commodity in the early days in the Southwest because materials and tools to work them were hard to come by. Even nails were so scarce that priests were told how many they were allowed to build their missions. Early hinges were made of wood or rawhide. There are few examples of ironwork that date to Spanish Colonial times, and decorative metal was almost nonexistent.

Nails, other hardware and the tools to work them became readily available after 1880, making building, locking and hinging objects much easier. Today, though ready-made is prevalent, there are many ironworkers in the area still hand-forging beautifully wrought hinges, door pulls and knockers.

For light, the early Indians and Spanish either worked outside by day, or inside by dim window and doorway light. Fuel for fires was scarce, and was usually conserved for cooking and winter heat. The Spanish did introduce candlemaking, but again, the materials were expensive, and most candles were saved for religious occasions. Kerosene, gas and electric lighting, and the fixtures that were needed for these, were introduced by the Anglos, and were not commonly in use until well into the twentieth century. The traditional center of Taos Pueblo still refuses electricity, and many rural communities have acquired it only recently.

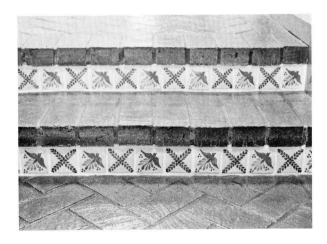

These brick hallway steps are highlighted with a row of colorful Mexican tiles between the risers.

Opposite, top row. Talavera tile sink with tile corners. Hand-painted Talavera tiles, Mexico, 4 x 4 inches. *Second row.* Hand-forged wrought-iron hinges, bolts, hasps, bosses and locks from throughout the Southwest. *Third row.* Hand-forged bull doorknocker, San Cristóbal de las Casas, Mexico, 4 1/2 inches long. Hand-forged cabinet pulls. Portion of hand-forged *reja*, 4 x 2 1/2 feet. *Bottom row.* Hand-punched tin light with hinged glass front, Mexico. *Estrella* (star) light, tin and glass, Mexico. Tin chandelier. Tin sconce with blown glass globe.

Italian tiles of various motifs are set into the wall around a wet bar.

Opposite, top left. Hand-painted Talavera tile sink and bathroom walls brighten this small half-bath.

Opposite, top right. The stove area of this Arizona kitchen becomes the focal point of the room with Talavera tiled arch and backboard.

Opposite, bottom left. Note the ceramic animal fireplace from Mexico, a charming feature of this bath area.

Painted tiles from Tonola, Mexico, are used to decorate this fireplace hearth.

Opposite, bottom right. The cleansing area of the Mosque in Abiquiu is decorated with Moorish tiles set in interesting geometric patterns.

A tile floor and tiled arch accent give this Taos doorway a Mexican flavor.

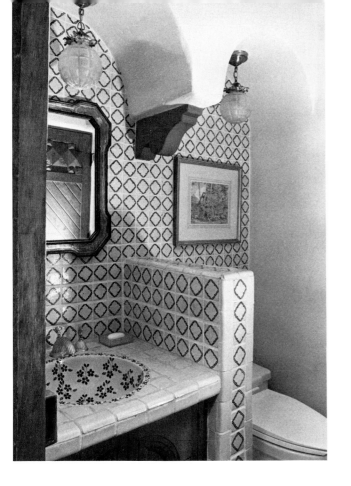

One family in San Cristóbal de las Casas, Mexico, makes these wonderful hand-forged, hand-stamped animal door knockers. The door is protected from the knocking feet by an iron *clavo* (nail).

"Gothic Study"—an iron door knocker made by Tom Joyce of Santa Fe.

Elk door knocker designed and hand-forged by Rolando de Leon of Santa Fe.

Wrought-iron scorpion door knocker from Mexico.

Hammered iron hinges on an early nineteenth-century door. Metal was rare in the early days; this iron could have been recycled from weapons or worn tools.

Metal door handle of simple and elegant design. The pattern of the punched metal is reminiscent of tooled Spanish leather.

Escutcheon lock with slender key-shaped latch on a plain Spanish Colonial chest.

Scorpion bolt from Mexico, made of hand-forged and hand-wrought iron.

Elaborate early Spanish Colonial escutcheon lock on an inlaid chest. The eighteenth-century owners of this piece would have been very wealthy to afford such fine work.

Three wrought-iron window grills (*rejas*) of varying design. Wrought iron was a late introduction to the Southwest, which became popular quickly. It is used for many purposes, decorative and protective, and has become a showcase for many creative ideas.

Hanging wooden candle holder at the Martinez Hacienda is an example of the earliest imported light fixtures. The Spanish brought candles and knowledge of candlemaking with them in the sixteenth century, but materials were rare and candles were used mostly in churches and the homes of the wealthy.

Candelabra of wood at Las Golondrinas. These hanging chandeliers were supported from a wooden pulley, with a rope attached to the wall to raise and lower the lights.

Colorful painted wood sideboard and elaborately stamped and shaped tinwork at Rancho de los Caballeros in Wickenburg, Arizona. A Mexican-Southwestern folk flavor is seen throughout the building.

One of the Spanish-introduced folk arts experiencing a revival is tinwork; this example from Taos features mirrors inset in a stamped tin wall sconce.

Tin chandelier with a glass-inlaid star hangs from a painted herringbone *latilla* ceiling. The lamp is a copy of a silver chandelier, modified only slightly to fit available materials.

A Mexican interpretation of a carriage light, adapted into an outside wall fixture. The metal casing is stamped, and a flower design is fashioned behind the light bulb.

Two bracketed lanterns from Mexico. These wrought-iron fixtures are popular in patios and outside areas throughout the Southwest.

Robert Woodman of Santa Fe was a popular tinsmith during the 1930s and 1940s. He designed many fixtures for local establishments and homes. This shaped and painted tin chandelier found its way to Phoenix, where it hangs over the dining-room table.

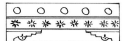

Posts, Corbels and Lintels

Posts evolved from plain log supports of the Indian and Spanish Colonial periods to the chamfered, spiral and turned posts of the twentieth century. Spiral posts were derived from Salomonic columns at St. Peter's in Rome and were copied all over Latin America in Colonial architecture.

Corbels are common in Islamic, Spanish and Mexican buildings and have been carved and decorated throughout the Southwest in a variety of designs since the Franciscan friars first showed the rosette and shell patterns to the local Indian laborers. During the Spanish and Mexican eras, corbels and beams were hand-adzed and silhouettes were cut with saws. The wood was often chip-carved and incised, then colored with natural earth dyes. Territorial posts and corbels were modeled after Victorian and Gothic Revival examples on the East Coast, and feature often elaborate carved decorations.

Carved rope design post set into a half-wall of mud-plastered adobe forms an elegant entry-way to the patio area.

Opposite, top. Corbel 6 feet 8 inches long and lintel on rope-carved round pine posts (6-foot centers). *Middle.* Eight pueblo-style half-corbel variations. *Bottom.* Chip-carved double corbel and lintel. Full corbel, decorative carving.

Corner post on the portal entrance to John and Barbara Brenner's Taos home.

Typical Territorial-style post, squared with a simple silhouette-carved design.

Rope-carved post, Taos. The rope design derived from Salomonic columns, used in St. Peter's in Rome, originally in Solomon's temple in Jerusalem.

This decorative post and carved corbel is now part of the wall enclosing the former portal. Two *ristras* of red chile pods hang from the viga ends.

Classic full corbel, chip-carved to appear hand-adzed.

Corner corbel.

Stepped corner corbel.

Details of an unusual portal lintel and corbel carved from one piece of wood.

Unusual corbel treatment, formed by two by four pine boards stacked in step design.

Ila McAfee designed and carved this corbel and lintel on her studio in Taos. The pack train of outlined burros adds a distinctive folk flavor to the exterior of the studio.

Ward Alan Minge says this corbel on his portal is an abstract apple tree design, with two fruits dangling on either end.

Carved full corbel and lintel with elegant scroll work.

Corbel bracket with routed outline carved around the saw-cut edges, which lends a more Mexican touch to the design.

Gothic Revival style corbeling details on a squared Territorial post. The design is typical of the folk adaptations of Eastern style found throughout the West.

Opposite, top. The singular lintel over the doorway to the San José de Gracia Church in Trampas, New Mexico. The central design is a sort of griffin/angel and the script around it reads in Spanish the date and the name of the carver —Nicolas B. Apadaca.

Opposite, bottom. The stepped wall of this adobe storefront was probably added in the 1940s in imitation of western wood facades. The corbels and lintel are hand-carved in a rough chip style.

A good-luck horseshoe hangs on this hand-cut corbel.

This gateway frames a lovely view of the fields and farms of the Taos Valley. The lintel piece supports a corbel laid "upside down" as a decorative touch.

Corbel bracket carved in an abstract bird design, with highlights etched in the wood with a router. Also note the hanging metal and glass fixture from Mexico.

An array of four carved and colorfully painted wood and plaster lintels from the Kachina Lodge in Taos. Built in the 1950s, the building reflects the revived interest in folk motif and personalized architectural detail.

Lintel at the Ila McAfee Studio in Taos, designed and carved by the artist, known for her paintings of landscapes and horses.

Hand-hewn lintel with additional sunburst carving. A good-luck horse-shoe hangs over the door to protect those that enter.

Carved by Nicolai Fechin, this rosette design on a keystone-shaped wooden lintel is unique.

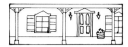

Portals

Portals protect walls and doorways from snow and rain, and provide shade on warm summer days. The early Indian and Spanish portals were wooden posts, usually forked at the top to hold crosspieces that supported brush thatching. Portals are usually situated within a courtyard or patio formed by the walls of a house. On a linear building, they are on the east or south side of the structure. If the building is L- or U-shaped, the portal is along the length of the inner walls, most often facing south.

Today, portals continue to be important entryways and covered areas, and some modern homes have enclosed portals that serve as a greenhouse area. Portals have as many variations as do the adobe buildings they decorate; each is a kind of signature or clue to the period and the tastes of the individual builder.

The portal at Las Palomas Educational Retreat Center, once the home of Mabel Dodge Luhan and her husband, Tony, and the site of many interesting visits by Mabel's friends, including D. H. Lawrence, Dorothy Brett, Witter Bynner and Martha Graham, among many other well-known writers, painters and *bons vivants.*

Opposite, top. Typical Territorial pitched roof adobe with narrow portal, 6 1/4 feet deep. The house is 14 x 49 feet with four rooms: living room 12 x 12 feet, bath 6 x 8 feet, and two bedrooms, each 12 x 12 feet. The walls are 14 inches thick.   Pueblo-style adobe, with 10-foot-deep portal on north side. The house is 20 x 50 feet and has three rooms. Living, dining and kitchen 17 1/2 x 30 feet, bedroom 17 1/2 x 12 feet, and bath 8 x 17 1/2 feet. The walls are 14 inches thick. *Middle.* Territorial-style portal, 6 feet deep with 6-inch-square posts, corbels 2 x 12 inches and scrolled trim board. Colonial pine bench, Taos Pueblo drum and Penasco-style door. Pine plank floor. *Bottom.* Pueblo-style portal, 10 feet deep, with corner fireplace, plum-colored flagstone floor, Mexican pigskin and cedar furniture, wrought-iron, and painted folk-style door. Corbels and lintels are chip carved and colored in the recessed areas.

The portal at Las Palomas as viewed from the inside.

The three-sided portal at the Blumenschein home in Taos, now part of the Kit Carson Foundation. Homes often expanded to U- or L-shaped structures as the family grew and rooms were added on.

Two views of a large south-facing portal in Nambe. The glass doors at the west end open into an enclosed greenhouse area that was the zaguán, or covered entryway. The unique feature of this portal is the lintel; it is over 30 feet long, and the five corbels are all carved from that one piece of timber.

Looking through a sculpted arch down the length of the portal of Edwin Bewley's home in Taos. Mr. Bewley purchased the home in 1957 (it dates from the 1800s) and added this portal with a sensitivity to the traditional style.

Territorial portal and entryway to the home of Dr. and Mrs. Albert Simms in Santa Fe. The lines are clean and simple, providing a traditional entry to their adobe dwelling.

The porch of the "Mora house" at Rancho de Las Golondrinas (La Cienega Village Museum) is named after a Northern New Mexico village where homes like this were common in the nineteenth century. The pitched roof is composed of overlapping boards, typical of structures in the snowy mountain country of the North. The posts are square, with designs cut in the wood, another folk adaptation of the Territorial style. A small herb garden is in front of the house.

A roadside cantina (bar) in Rodarte, New Mexico, with painted folk murals, including this landscape with burros loaded with wood and a dancing girl advertizing "Santa Fe Wine." Murals were (and still are) important expressions of creativity; some in Santa Fe have strong political messages, many depict historical or religious scenes, and others are simply decorative.

The two-story portal of Jean and Oliver Seth's home in Santa Fe; the upper posts, corbels and lintels mirror those below. A St. Francis by Tesuque wood-carver Ben Ortega greets visitors, and a Mexican wrought-iron "tree of life" hangs above the dark plastered protective dado. The sign above the door reads "Mil Cumbres" (a thousand hills), referring to the 360-degree view the house offers.

Portal in the inner courtyard of the Ward Alan Minge home. Part of the house foundations date to a Piro pueblo occupied from the thirteenth century. The house was permanently settled and constructed in the 1700s by the family of Felipe Gutierrez, one of the original petitioners to the Spanish Crown for the Bernalillo town grant in 1704.

L-shaped mountain-style Territorial portal of classic detail and dimension.

The portal of the Martin home in El Rito, New Mexico, is an example of New Mexico Territorial-style building detail. The proportions are classic, and the details are typical. The roof planks run the entire length of the portal, in Eastern U.S. fashion. The house dates to at least 1850, and was the home of Venceslao and Cleofas Jaramillo. Cleofas founded the Folklorica Society for the recording and preservation of Spanish folk life as well as writing books *Shadows of the Past* and *Memories of a Young Girl.*

Ornate gingerbread detailing highlights this Queen Anne style portal in Pojoaque, New Mexico.

The second-story porch of the Felipe B. Delgado house in Santa Fe, built in 1890 and remodeled in Victorian style after the Civil War.

This Tubac, Arizona, building features a narrow open portal that could be thatched with brush for shade. This building dates to the 1950s, but Tubac's history dates to prehistoric times, with many Indian sites. The Spanish established a northern presidio, or fort, here in 1752.

A 1920s photo of a portal in California. The decor is distinctly Southwestern, but the architecture reflects the California Mission style with its white walls and tiled roof. *Photo, courtesy Museum of New Mexico, neg number 108323.* 237

These adobe arches and covered portal in Arizona provide a cool shaded outdoor area. Wide covered walkways are common in ecclesiastical architecture
in the desert regions of the West and Southwest.

Patios

Patios or central open areas have always been a part of southwestern architecture. Indian pueblos had central plazas where trade was conducted and where outside cooking, socializing and ceremonial activities took place.

Spanish villages also had a main plaza area, and Spanish haciendas enclosed a central *placita*. Plazas were used for all sorts of outside activities, summer living areas and, in times of attack, as a protected corral area for valuable livestock. Entrance to and from *placitas* was by means of a zaguán, which was a covered passageway with heavy protective gates leading to the inner compound. The family or community well was usually safely located within this protected area.

Anglo settlers used patio areas primarily for social activities and began to incorporate elaborate flower gardens in these enclosed exterior spaces.

The twelve-room Kit Carson house in Taos dating from 1825 was built around a central patio area. The *placita* was used for many outdoor activities, including baking. Note the adobe *horno* next to the covered well.

The de la Peña house in Santa Fe was built in 1845. The original home was only four rooms, but by 1887 when Francisco de la Peña died the house had grown to accommodate eight children. The property was divided in 1909 among the six surviving children. Each received a portion of the land, six vigas of the house, and free entrance and exit to it. Artist Frank Applegate added the second-story portal and balconies when he purchased the house in 1917.

One of two *placitas* in the Martinez Hacienda in Taos; the water well was located within the protective walls of the home. The Martinez Hacienda, now part of the Kit Carson Foundation, represents the Spanish Colonial Period from about 1804 to 1827. Oxcarts loaded with goods from the Chihuahua trade stopped here regularly.

Artist Cady Wells bought an old adobe north of Santa Fe in the 1920s and had architect John Gaw Meem remodel it in classic Territorial style. This formal, bricked patio space is a shady and pleasant garden area. Visible under the portal is part of Wells' extensive collection of Spanish Colonial folk art, now in the collection of the Museum of International Folk Art in Santa Fe. *Photo by Tyler Dingee, ca. 1950, courtesy Museum of New Mexico, neg number 59486.*

South-facing portal and patio area in Nambe. The multileveled garden and seating areas command a spectacular view of the Sangre de Cristo Mountains to the east.

A Mexican-styled patio in Phoenix; the focal point of this entry area is a Mexican tiled fountain, surrounded by flowers. The patio also features a tiled *banco* built into the wall, and an earth-colored tile floor.

Opposite, patio of the Heard Museum of Phoenix. The Museum contains major collections of American Indian Art, including the Barry Goldwater collection of Hopi kachinas and the Fred Harvey Collection of Indian Art and artifacts from the Harvey chain of railroad hotels. The bronze sculpture of a Navajo shepherdess with her flock is by Apache artist Allan Houser.

This formal garden contains several seating and entertaining areas. Small adobe walls meander throughout the grassy lawn and garden areas as a visual link to the spacious adobe home in downtown Santa Fe.

This Pueblo-style portal features a staircase to the second-story balcony. The stepped wall, painted *nicho* and dark plaster dado are all elements of the Pueblo style.

A sculptural adobe wall echos the risers on this outside staircase. Note the small shuttered window with wooden bars.

This adobe dome at Tumacacori, Arizona, has sculpted adobe steps built into the dome, possibly for access to the bell tower; they provide an interesting visual pattern.

Mabel Dodge Luhan placed these decorative pots on the stairs outside one of her Pueblo-style homes in Taos. Pots were sometimes used as chimney pieces, but this is a unique application.

Two examples of the decorative and functional use of ladders. Once the only means of access to many homes, ladders are now a popular decorative element in many Pueblo and Territorial-style homes.

Wooden spindles decorate the half-wall of this outside staircase in Taos. Note the viga ends that form sunburst patterns below the round landing.

Staircase leading to a second-story sleeping porch at the Mabel Dodge Luhan complex in Taos. The soft lines of the stair walls complement the curved walls of the building.

Fences and Outside Walls

Early Indian and Spanish homes formed their own outside walls and defined a living area by the town layout, which enclosed a central plaza. Garden areas were probably first protected by naturally encouraged growths of cactus or other thorny weeds. Today, outside walls and fences are constructed from all types of native materials. As well as being protective, they define outside living areas and can help to make a small house seem larger, or visually connect a large house to its site. Walls and fences also screen out unwanted views and insulate a home from street noises.

The mysterious and enigmatic adobe wall that surrounds the churchyard of the San Estevan del Rey Mission Church at Acoma, New Mexico. *Photographed in 1935 by T. Harmon Parkhurst, courtesy Museum of New Mexico, neg number 1987.*

Opposite, top. Pueblo-style home, Santa Fe, aspen pole and adobe wall. *Middle.* Hacienda-style home with rooms around central courtyard. Zaguán gate with pediment. Two-story pueblo-style home, Taos, with low wall and carved gate. *Bottom.* Stepped wall entrance to a large adobe estate.

Triple corbel entry in Corrales, New Mexico; corbel brackets were placed at right angles to one another to form this unusual gateway.

This wall in Tubac, Arizona, was built with ample room around the branches of a growing tree.

248

Adobe arches and mud-plastered walls become a sculpted exterior for this traditional-style home.

This fence, built of dead-standing aspen, is popularly called a "coyote fence" because it keeps animals out. The fence also serves as an effective visual screen; in this case, a building is concealed while the view of Taos Mountain remains complete.

Arched garden entrance; a beautiful garden in Taos is enclosed with this rounded and curvilinear adobe wall.

Coyote fence with adobe pillars. Many materials can be used to make these popular fences—downed aspen, cedar or, as in the example below, cactus.

This fence in Tubac, Arizona, constructed from living trees interlaced with fallen wood, provides an effective barrier.

Perhaps the most effective deterrent of all, this coyote fence is made from cactus. There is evidence that some of the early Pueblo peoples may have cultivated living cactus barriers around their defensive clifftop sites.

Stone foundations support these multileveled garden walls in Santa Fe. Lace ivy and spindled doors also help to decorate the length of the walls.

These walls surrounding the former Mabel Dodge estate in Taos provide a sense of fluidity as well as imparting a soft sculptural feeling inherent in pueblo-style architecture.

An adobe arch set into a coyote fence is the frame for this charming paneled gate. Mexican tile house numbers are set into the wall, and large ceramic pots are set on either side.

Gates

Spanish settlements had large defensive gates called *portones*. These were huge double doors wide enough for oxcarts and farm wagons, and often included a small door for pedestrian use. Smaller wooden gates and garden gates became popular after 1900 and were first made from old Colonial doors that were salvaged and cut to half size. Wrought-iron gates were introduced by 1910, but the most commonly seen gates are still made from wood. Most gates are painted, carved, spindled or decorated in some fanciful way.

The entrance to the Martinez Hacienda near Taos is one of the few surviving examples of a defensive *placita*-type structure. The large hacienda gates, called *portones* in Spanish, could be opened for wagons or to herd livestock into the protected patio area when necessary.

Opposite, top. GARDEN GATES. Rosette carved in pine, 1/4-inch relief. Geometric wood overlay. Cedar and pine butterfly motif overlay. Painted gate with spindle center window. All approximately 3 feet 4 inches x 2 feet. *Middle.* ENTRY GATES. Raised panel and hand-painted santos (San Pascual, St. Francis, Santo Niño, Guadalupe). Decorative spindle on pine door. Animal jigsaw cut overlay in pine 2 x 12 inches. All approximately 5 x 2 1/2 feet. *Bottom.* Contemporary adaptation of double folk Territorial entry gates. Moldings and raised panels form cross and double cross designs; approximately 6 x 5 feet.

Two gates from Las Palomas in Taos, the estate of Mabel Dodge Luhan. The large entry gates have raised carved panels. A bell hangs in the sculpted adobe wall above the lintel. Bells were treasured objects in the early days.

Simple paneled gates from an old farm in the Nambe valley. The gates are wide enough for a wagon to pass through, and can be closed when protection is needed.

Classic Territorial-style gates in Pojoaque, New Mexico. The cutout designs and add-on molding is typical Penasco style.

Small garden gate with simple wood spindles. The steps are locally quarried limestone, containing many small fossils.

A high adobe wall encloses this spindled gate. A *ristra* of red chile, a popular fall decoration, hangs by the gate.

Stepped adobe walls with raised sculpted arches enclose the front patio of the lovely Hughston home in Taos.

Aspen wood tied together forms this garden gate in a low adobe arch at the Taos Book Shop.

American Indian motifs of clouds, rain, mountains and a plumed serpent are painted on this garden gate in Taos.

Pueblo Indian dancers (one with gourd rattle, the other holding a sacred spruce branch) are carved on this gate on Camino del Monte Sol in Santa Fe. Along this street many of the early artists built their homes in the 1920s and 1930s.

Behind this simple gate is one of the few remaining Northern New Mexico Territorial homes with a pitched board roof.

Small side gate at the Museum of Fine Arts in Santa Fe. Though the building is not adobe, its rounded shapes evoke that organic medium.

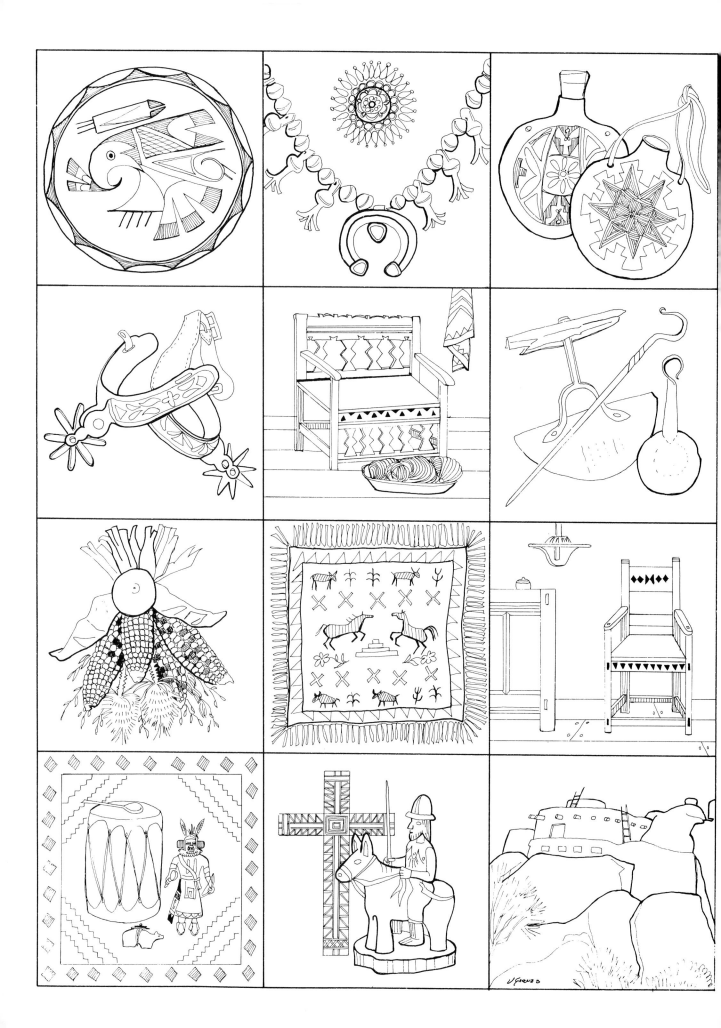

Other Wonderful Things

In this section we include some of the special objects that caught our eyes as we were working on this project; it is an eclectic and very personalized selection of arts, crafts and architectural elements that did not fit elsewhere in the book, but somehow belonged.

Below left. An oxcart used in the Chihuhua trade throughout the eighteenth century. The wheels are cut from one piece of wood and attached to the wooden axle with a peg. This example is in the Martinez Hacienda in Taos. There is one person, Joe Graves of Taos, who still makes these wagons as reproductions for museums and private collectors. *Below right.* Pigeons roosting on one of the cupolas of the Ranchos de Taos Church, a favorite spot.

Dovecotes at Las Palomas in Taos. *Paloma* is Spanish for dove, and these are the homes for the namesake of the educational institution in Taos, which is housed in the former estate of Mabel Dodge Luhan.

Opposite, top row. Sitkiyaki revival design bowl from Tewa Village, Hopi. Navajo squash-blossom necklace of silver and turquoise. Zuni inlaid pin, silver and turquoise. Acoma pottery canteens, Mary S. Torvino, 6 x 4 inches. *Second row.* Silver inlaid spurs, Mexico. Copy of Spanish Colonial bench, 3 feet x 4 inches. Spanish Colonial food chopper, flat spoon and wrought-iron spike. *Third row.* Wall hanging of Indian corn, gourds, grasses and red chile, Sopyn Fruit Stand, Rinconada, New Mexico. Colcha embroidery, Frances Graves, Taos. Spanish Colonial chair with shelf *(repiza)* above. *Bottom row.* Taos Pueblo cottonwood drum, Zuni bear fetish, and Hopi badger kachina on Navajo rug background. Santiago carved by Gloria Lopez, Cordova, New Mexico. Empie dwelling near Scottsdale, Arizona.

Well house at Rancho de Las Golondrinas (Sparrow Ranch) in the La Cienega Village Museum. *Ciénega* means spring, and spring water was obtained from this cupola-covered well for many years.

Cottonwood bucket carved from one piece of wood.

The "Molino de Sapello" at Las Golondrinas. This adobe flour mill was moved to the outdoor museum in the 1970s and is still put to use during annual fall and spring open houses.

Hanging shelf carved from pine surrounded by other wonderful objects, including a bread paddle for reaching into an adobe *horno*, a strand of garlic, a tin candle holder and a handmade child's chair.

Carved and painted giraffes by folk artist Felipe Archuleta of Tesuque graze in the trees of Elaine and Arnold Horwitch's Santa Fe home.

A carved stone lion's head emerges from the adobe wall of the San Xavier Church near Tucson.

Old ceramic pots hang in the beaver tail cactus and paloverde tree forest of a Tucson home.

Unusual door bell, literally an array of five bells with a handle for turning them.

Other Wonderful Things
Home of Bill and Sunnie Empie

We wanted to include the Empie dwelling here, as a focus of our "Other Wonderful Things" chapter because we felt it warranted special attention as a successful architectural statement. The Empies themselves call it a "rhythmic curvilinear desert abstraction" and a "live-in sculpture, a functional sculpture," and these are perfect descriptions of the home and its setting in the Precambrian boulders that once sheltered Hohokam Indians as long ago as 1250.

The dwelling is not built of adobe, because of the strict codes in the Phoenix area, but it incorporates the essence of an earth-sensitive medium like adobe, and does an exceptional job blending into the landscape as an organic presence. The day we took photographs there, five hawks stood on the boulders of the dwelling, as sort of guardian good omens and symbols of the power of the place itself.

The Empie dwelling is north of Scottsdale in the desert foothill country of Arizona. The architect was Charles F. Johnson of Santa Fe.

A granite boulder merges with the walls to form the fireplace in the master bedroom. The mantel is sculpted to echo the stone, and the arched fireplace opening has a rounded sculptural edge.

A young hawk roosts on the granite boulders that are a part of the Empie dwelling. Hawks are thought by many to be a good omen. They return to the same nesting grounds each year, passing the sites on to future hawk generations. Saguaro cactus stand in the foreground.

As one approaches the Empie dwelling one sees only the natural boulders first; the building seems just to rest within the rock.

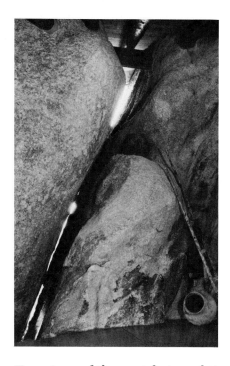

Two views of the west-facing solstice window in the living room. Solstice marks the time when the sun is farthest from the Equator, an important occurrence marked by people throughout the world.

The living room with its central shepherd's-bed fireplace and covered *banco* area. Rounded shapes are everywhere, and one can see the granite wall of the dining room beyond.

Interior view of the front door and stepped entryway. The bronze Allan Houser sculpture seems made for the shaped *banco* on which it rests. The windows in the dwelling are all thermopane, and are set into grooves in the boulders and sealed with silicone. The edges are disguised with powdered stone grout. *Below.* The living room of the Empie dwelling. The entire west wall is boulders, with narrow window openings in the curves of the stones. An Indian-style ladder rests against the rock. The floor is poured concrete, tinted in an earth tone. The vigas that support the roof are set almost a foot into the boulders.

During construction a Hohokam firepit and three pots were unearthed; the Empies preserved them, and incorporated the prehistoric firepit into the guest room fireplace. Careful not to disturb the original firepit, they constructed the newer one to the right; the chimney opening is a natural crevice between the stones.

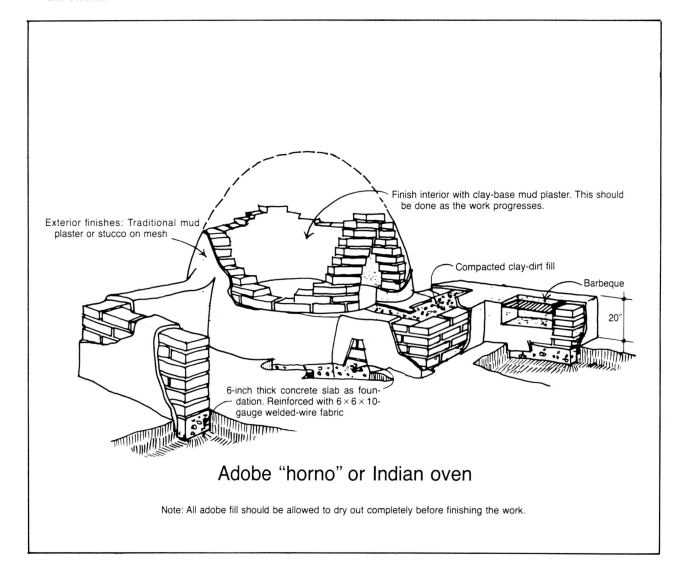

Exterior finishes: Traditional mud plaster or stucco on mesh

Finish interior with clay-base mud plaster. This should be done as the work progresses.

Compacted clay-dirt fill

Barbeque

20"

6-inch thick concrete slab as foundation. Reinforced with 6 × 6 × 10-gauge welded-wire fabric

Adobe "horno" or Indian oven

Note: All adobe fill should be allowed to dry out completely before finishing the work.

Construction Details and Floor Plans

TRADITIONAL INTERIOR MUD PLASTER (preferably adobe walls have "settled" for 3 to 6 months, 1/4 to 1/2 inch settlement factor). *First Rough Coat:* Apply to moistened wall a mud plaster mix of 4 parts screened adobe dirt, 1 part plaster sand, and 1 part finely chopped straw. (This coat will crack.) *Second Coat* (often the "final" coat): Apply to moistened wall a mud plaster mix of *equal* parts screened adobe dirt (a colored dirt if desired), plaster sand (in northern New Mexico "Pilar" sand), and finely chopped straw. (This coat will not crack.) TRADITIONAL INTERIOR WALL FINISHES: *Straw Showing:* Wash (with pressure) the final, partially dry coat of mud plaster with a burlap rag, smoothing any hairline cracks or uneven areas. The straw will "shine" when dry. *Slip Coat:* To dry a wall, apply (with a sponge, piece of sheepskin or piece of burlap) a thin, soupy wash of *finely* screened, colored earth. ALTERNATIVE INTERIOR WALL FINISHES: *Transparent Protective Sealer:* A nonglossy protective finish, not altering the natural color of the bricks, may be obtained by applying a clear acrylic sealer or a silicone masonry sealer. For harder, tougher interior surfaces, paint with raw linseed oil. This imparts a richer, darker color. Allow at least two weeks for curing. *Paint:* Acrylic latex flat exterior paint or alkyd resin oil base exterior masonry paint. No prime coat required. *Cement Wash:* Brush onto a moistened surface a wash of Medusa or White Cement and water (paint consistency). After initial set, this prime coat should be fogged with water several times daily, until the cement is fully set and hardened. A second application of cement wash, tinted with pigment if desired, may be applied as a final coat. (This finish is more common in Arizona applications.) *Cement or Structolyte Finish:* Chicken wire or stucco netting is fastened to the walls with furring nails driven into the bricks (metal lath is attached to wood surfaces that have been covered with 15 or 30 number felt paper). Cement is applied in scratch, brown, and finish coats according to standard practice. Structolyte is applied in either one or two coats, depending on the plasterer's skill.

Construction details included are generalized for use with most adobe projects and are included as guidelines for the builder. Local, state and national building codes must be consulted and observed.

Edward W. Smith of Tesuque, New Mexico, author of *Adobe Bricks in New Mexico,* circular 188, New Mexico Bureau of Mines and Mineral Resources, an excellent reference on adobes, thoughtfully allowed us to use construction detail drawings (*horno,* page 268, drawings pages 270–273, and information on wall finishes (linseed oil and cement wash), which he obtained from the California Research Corporation report of 1963. These construction detail drawings were made by Dale Zinn, an architect with Architecture Planning Group, Santa Fe. Architects William Lumpkins also of Santa Fe and Allen McNown of Nambe reviewed the drawings.

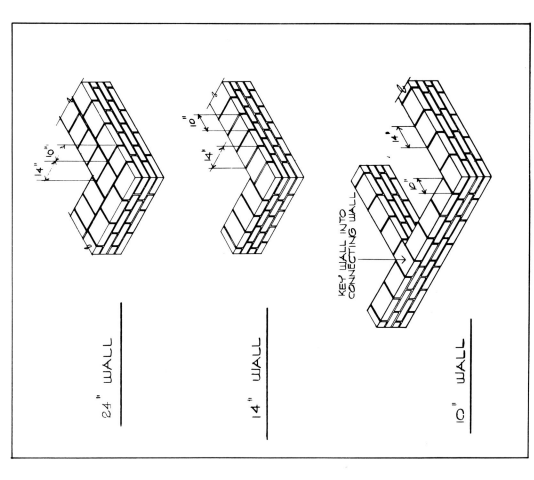

24" WALL

14" WALL

10" WALL

KEY WALL INTO CONNECTING WALL

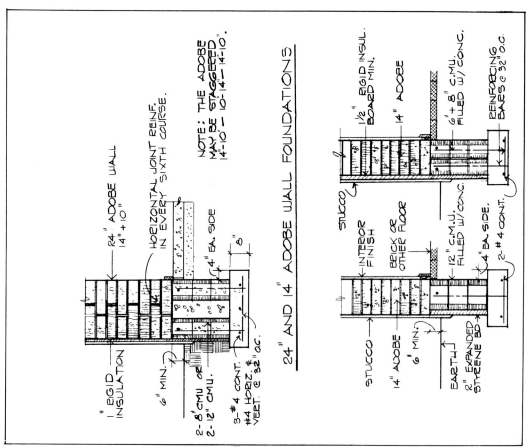

24" AND 14" ADOBE WALL FOUNDATIONS

1" RIGID INSULATION

24" ADOBE WALL 14" + 10"

HORIZONTAL JOINT REINF. IN EVERY SIXTH COURSE.

NOTE: THE ADOBE MAY BE STAGGERED 14-10 — 10-14— 14-10.

6" MIN.

4" EA. SIDE

8"

2- 8" CMU OR 2- 12" CMU.

3- #4 CONT. #4 HORIZ. & VERT. @ 32" O.C.

STUCCO

INTERIOR FINISH

1½" RIGID INSUL. BOARD MIN.

14" ADOBE

BRICK OR OTHER FLOOR

6" + 8" C.M.U. FILLED W/ CONC.

STUCCO

14" ADOBE

12" C.M.U. FILLED W/ CONC.

REINFORCING BARS @ 32" O.C.

EARTH

2" EXPANDED STYRENE BD.

6" MIN.

4" EA. SIDE

2- #4 CONT.

24- and 14-inch adobe wall foundations. Foundations should be at least 16 inches wide and rest on undisturbed earth at a point below the frost line. Perimeter insulation is required in New Mexico. *Right.* Standard adobe walls. Either cement or mud mortar can be effectively used, but if mud is chosen, it is advisable to allow every 4 vertical feet (approximately 12 courses up) to set for a few days to a week, depending on weather. The maximum height of a bearing wall is 10 times the width of the unit (adobe) being used. Adobe walls that are to be insulated should have the insulation fitted to the exterior to maintain the thermal-mass effect of the adobe.

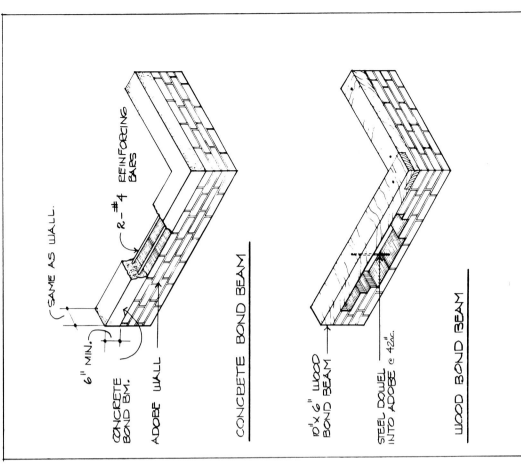

SAME AS WALL.

6" MIN.

2-#4 REINFORCING BARS

CONCRETE BOND BM.

ADOBE WALL

CONCRETE BOND BEAM

10"×6" WOOD BOND BEAM

STEEL DOWEL INTO ADOBE @ 42o.c.

WOOD BOND BEAM

Bond beams, wood timber and concrete. For wood bond beams, treated wood is often required, and joints are to be lapped a minimum of 6 inches.

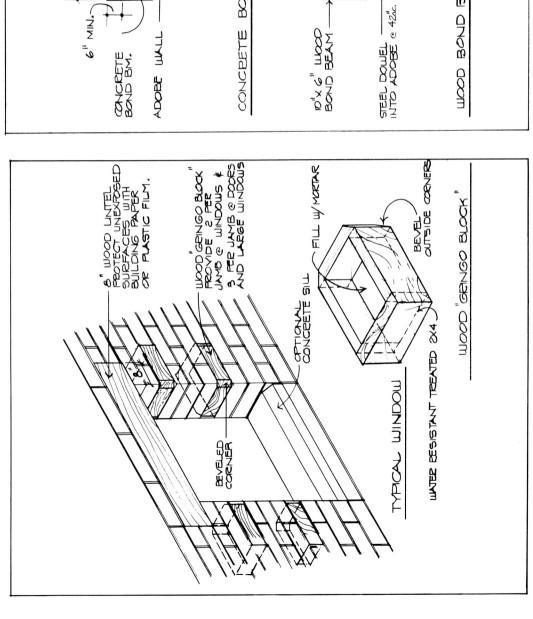

8" WOOD LINTEL PROTECT UNEXPOSED SURFACES WITH BUILDING PAPER OR PLASTIC FILM.

WOOD "GRINGO BLOCK" PROVIDE 2 PER JAMB @ WINDOWS & 3 PER JAMB @ DOORS AND LARGE WINDOWS

OPTIONAL CONCRETE SILL

BEVELED CORNER

TYPICAL WINDOW

WATER RESISTANT TREATED 2×4

FILL W/MORTAR

BEVEL OUTSIDE CORNERS

WOOD "GRINGO BLOCK"

Window opening detail. Lintels should extend 1 1/2 feet onto the adobe wall past the opening on both sides, and be the full width of the wall.

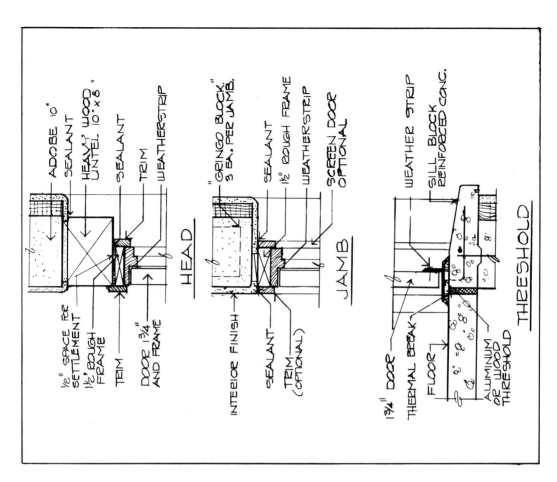

Door installation detail.

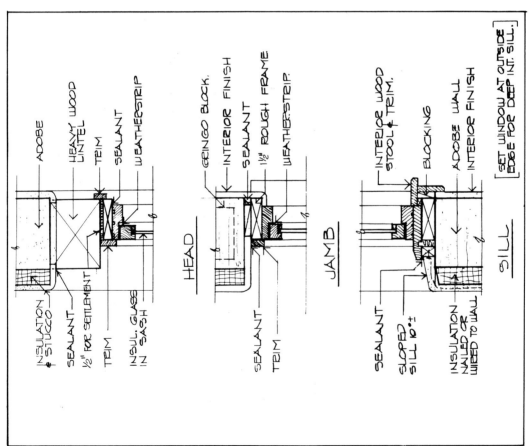

Window installation detail.

272

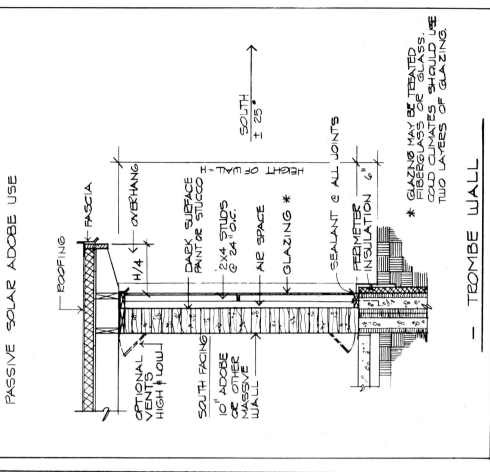

PASSIVE SOLAR ADOBE USE

— TROMBE WALL —

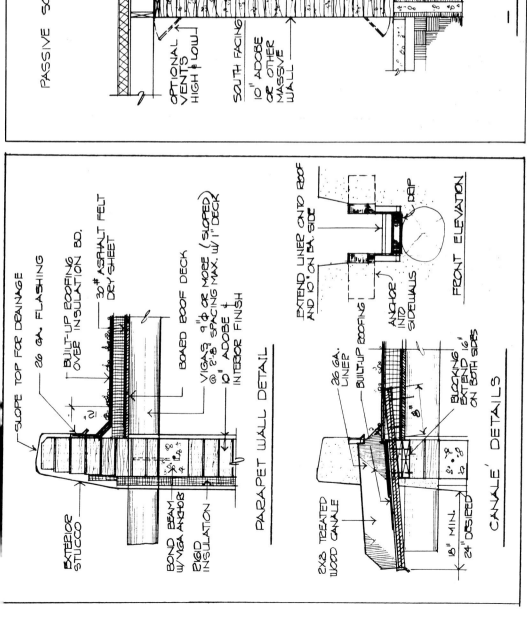

PARAPET WALL DETAIL

CANALE' DETAILS

FRONT ELEVATION

Parapet wall ("firewall") detail and *canale* details. The roofing and insulation method illustrated here is only one option. For a *latilla*, split cedar, saguaro or willow ceiling, a "double roof" is required because of the uneven nature of the materials that span the vigas. Joists 2 x 6 inches to 2 x 12 inches (depending on the amount of insulation desired), fiberglass (or other) insulation and plywood (or other) decking forms the second roof. A "double roof" allows for the viga/*latilla* ceiling to be flat for a traditional interior appearance, and the second roof to slope to allow for drainage.

Firewalls can be constructed to disguise this slope. *Right.* Passive solar Trombe wall. The airspace between the glazing and the adobe wall (4 inches) is a critical factor, as too much space causes heat to convect within the Trombe wall and negates the thermosiphoning effect desired for heating the room. For a more traditional appearance, small paned windows can be substituted for larger sheets of glass (with insignificant loss of solar gain).

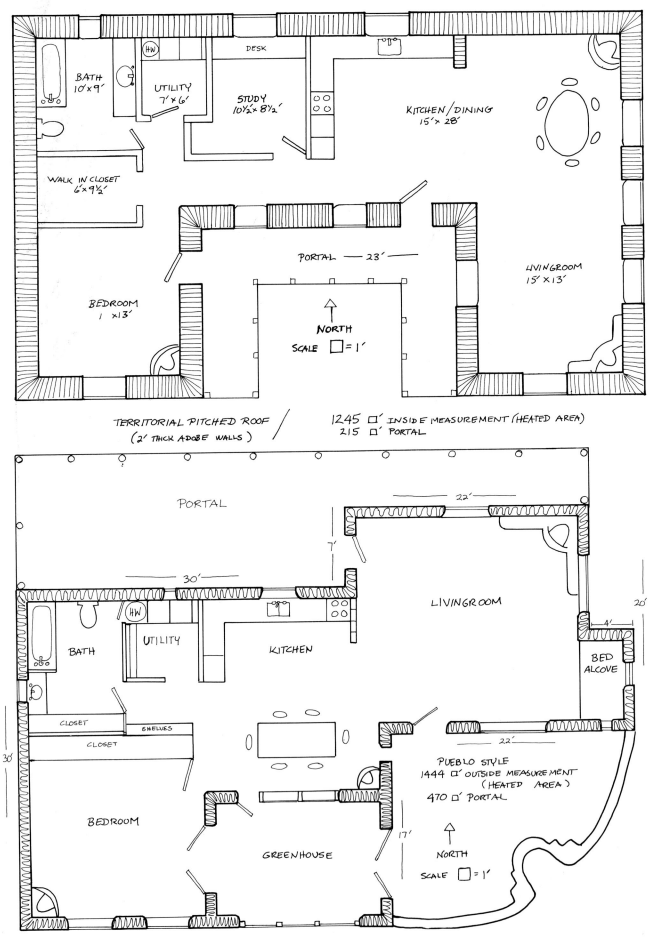

BATH
10' x 9'

UTILITY
7' x 6'

HW

DESK

STUDY
10½' x 8½'

KITCHEN/DINING
15' x 28'

WALK IN CLOSET
6' x 9½'

PORTAL — 23'

LIVINGROOM
15' x 13'

BEDROOM
1' x 13'

NORTH

SCALE ▢ = 1'

TERRITORIAL PITCHED ROOF
(2' THICK ADOBE WALLS)

1245 ▢' INSIDE MEASUREMENT (HEATED AREA)
215 ▢' PORTAL

PORTAL

22'

7'

LIVINGROOM

30'

HW

UTILITY

KITCHEN

4'

20'

BATH

BED
ALCOVE

CLOSET

SHELVES

CLOSET

22'

30'

PUEBLO STYLE
1444 ▢' OUTSIDE MEASUREMENT
(HEATED AREA)
470 ▢' PORTAL

BEDROOM

17'

GREENHOUSE

NORTH

SCALE ▢ = 1'

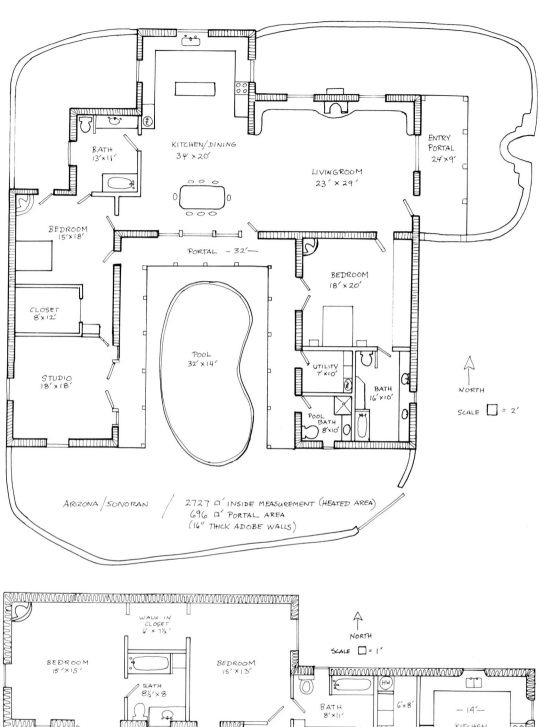

BATH
13'×11'

KITCHEN/DINING
34'×20'

LIVINGROOM
23'×29'

ENTRY
PORTAL
24'×9'

BEDROOM
15'×18'

PORTAL — 32'—

BEDROOM
18'×20'

CLOSET
8'×12'

POOL
32'×14'

UTILITY
7'×10'

BATH
16'×10'

STUDIO
18'×18'

POOL
BATH
8'×10'

NORTH

SCALE ☐ = 2'

ARIZONA/SONORAN / 2727 ☐' INSIDE MEASUREMENT (HEATED AREA)
696 ☐' PORTAL AREA
(16" THICK ADOBE WALLS)

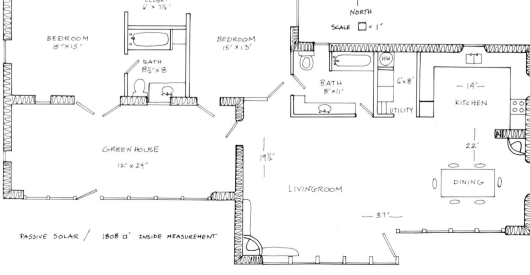

WALK IN
CLOSET
6'×7½'

NORTH

SCALE ☐ = 1'

BEDROOM
15'×15'

BEDROOM
15'×13'

BATH
8½'×8

BATH
8'×11'

HW

6'×8'

KITCHEN
—14'—

UTILITY

22'

GREEN HOUSE
12'×24'

19½'

LIVINGROOM

DINING

—37'—

PASSIVE SOLAR / 1808 ☐' INSIDE MEASUREMENT

Glossary

ACEQUIA: Irrigation ditch.

ADOBERO: One who works with adobe.

ADOBE: A brick of sun-dried earth, usually stabilized with straw or other material; a mixture of clay and silt deposits found in the basin areas of the Southwest United States, used to produce sun-dried bricks; a structure made of adobe bricks.

ALACENA: A built-in cabinet.

ALISAR: To smooth, to polish, to slip-coat with a colored mud wash.

BALUSTER: An upright support of a rail in a staircase, balcony, etc.

BANCO: A sculpted bench, often set into the wall or formed from the wall.

BOSS: Stud or decorative surround of a nail head.

BARRIO: A neighborhood.

BRACKET: An overhanging member projecting from a wall to support weight falling from outside the wall, or a similar piece to strengthen an angle.

BULLNOSE PLASTER: Plaster shaped in a curve around window and door openings.

BULTO: Carved and painted representation of a saint, usually three-dimensional.

CAMINO: Street.

CAMINO REAL: The trail from Mexico north, Royal Highway.

CANALE: Water spout, for roof drainage.

CANTINA: Bar.

CARIZZO: Cane, from a reed grass of the genus *Phragmites*.

CASA: House.

COLCHA: Decorative embroidery stitch, common in Spanish Colonial textiles; also the finished embroidery.

CIÉNEGA: Spring, marsh.

CLAVO: Nail.

CONCHA: Shell-shaped plaster ornamentation; also, the shape common in Navajo jewelry.

CORBEL: A projection from the face of a wall, supporting a weight or short timber placed lengthwise under a girder to afford a bearing.

CORNICE: The horizontal member that crowns a composition or facade.

DADO: The lower part of a wall when specially decorated.

DAUB: A rough coating of clay mortar applied by hand or trowel to both sides of a supporting framework of lathing or brushwork to form the wall.

DENTIL: A small rectangular block in a series projecting from a wall like teeth, as under a cornice.

ENCALAR: To whitewash.

ENJARRADORA: Plasterer.

EQUIPALE: Pigskin and cedar furniture from Jalisco, Mexico, which dates to the time of Cortés (1500s).

ESCUTCHEON: Metal shield around a keyhole, usually ornamental as well as protective.

ESTRELLA: Star; light fixture in the form of a star.

FETISH: An object believed to have special power.

FOGÓN: Fireplace, furnace, hearth.

GOLONDRINA: Swallow, the bird.

GRANERO: Grain chest.

JACAL: A construction method whereby walls are built of upright poles or sticks covered and chinked with mud.

JASPÉ: Gypsum, chalk, homemade whitewash.

HACIENDA: Large house.

HOGAN: Navajo dwelling constructed of jacal.

HORNO: Outdoor beehive-shaped baking oven.

KACHINA: A Pueblo Indian representation of a supernatural Being regarded as a messenger for human prayers; also, a carving of the Spirit or Deity.

KIVA: Native American religious structure, often subterranean and round.

LATILLA: Small pole used as lath in ceilings, or one of a series of poles, usually aspen, in a fence.

MANTA DE TECHO: Cotton muslin tacked on the ceiling, under the vigas to catch dust.

MOLINO: Mill.

MORADA: Worship house for the Penitente Brotherhood.

MOSQUE: Islamic church.

NICHO: Small niche carved into the adobe wall.

OCOTILLO: Native thorny desert shrub, also known as candlewood.

OLLA: Pot or pottery.

PALOMA: Dove.

PADERCITA: Small wall, usually stepped.

PEDIMENT: Decoration over portico, doorway or window.

PENITENTE: A Roman Catholic religious brotherhood.

PETROGLYPH: Design carved into a rock face.

PICTOGRAPH: Painted design on a rock face.

PLACITA: Fortified place, small town, court or patio.

PLAZA: The central area in a town, town square.

PORTAL: A porch or large roofed outside area adjacent to the house.

PORTÓN: Large gate, especially to a hacienda.

POSTIGO: Small opening in a door of a larger size.

PRESIDIO: A group of citizens armed for defense, an outpost fort.

PUDDLED ADOBE: Method of building with mud where layers are built up slowly directly on the wall and left to dry between courses.

QUEMADO: A sun-dried adobe brick that has undergone a modified low firing process, burnt adobe.

RAMMED EARTH: A method of constructing earth walls by placing moistened soil into forms and ramming it into place, after which the forms are removed, also known as pisé construction.

REJA: Window grating or railing, usually wrought iron.

REPIZA: Shelf, ledge, sill.

RETABLO: A two-dimensional painting of a saint or holy person, usually on a flat board.

SAGUARO: Native large cactus of the Sonoran desert.

SALA: Parlor, large room.

SANEFA: Painted border or stripe on the bottom part of a wall, also stencil.

SANTO: Image or statue of a saint or holy person.

SAVINO: Latilla made of unsplit juniper, cane or ocotillo.

SELENITE: Translucent mineral.

SITKIYAKI: Prehistoric proto-Hopi Pueblo, known for its fine pottery.

TABLA: Rough-hewn roof planking, board.

TABLITA: Pueblo Indian dance headdress made of wood, often in a stepped cloud pattern.

TERRONE: "Turtle back," a building block of earth cut directly from the marsh-grass swamps and dried in the same way as an adobe brick. Used particularly along the Rio Grande near Albuquerque.

THERMOPANE: Vacuum-sealed insulating window, usually double glazed.

TIERRA AMARILLA: Yellow earth.

TIERRA AZUL: Blue earth.

TIERRA BAYITA: Tan earth.

TIERRA BLANCA: White earth, usually micaceous.

TORREÓN: Tower, often defensive.

TRASTERO: Cupboard, china closet, upright cabinet.

TROMBE WALL: A solar window-box structure built against a dark-painted south-facing adobe wall, which performs as a thermosiphoning air collector. Named for Professor Felix Trombe.

VIGA: Horizontal roof beam, a round timber.

WAINSCOT: The lower three or four feet of a wall when finished differently from the remainder of the wall.

WATTLE AND DAUB: A structure composed of a vertical framework of woven twigs and thin poles on which mud is plastered.

ZAGUÁN: Covered entrance between the outside and an enclosed patio.

ZAMBULLO: Early New Mexican term for a handmade door with a pintle (wooden-pegged) hinge.

ZAPATA: Corbel.

Guide to Adobe Public Buildings

We include here a personal list of special places, open to the public, where one can see wonderful examples of architecture and art.

Indian Ruins
Arizona: Canyon de Chelly National Monument, Chinle
Casa Grande, near Phoenix
Navajo National Monument, near Kayenta
Montezuma Castle National Monument, near Flagstaff
Colorado: Hovenweep National Monument, Northwest of Cortez
Mesa Verde National Park, near Cortez
New Mexico: Aztec Ruins National Monument, Aztec
Bandelier National Monument, Los Alamos
Chaco Canyon National Monument, north of Gallup
Pecos National Monument, Pecos

Indian Pueblos
Indian Pueblos are located along the Rio Grande from Taos to south of Albuquerque, and west as far as Arizona. Visit these with the respect you would have visiting anyone's home. Listed here is a partial list of these wonderful villages.
Arizona: Hopi Reservation, First, Second and Third Mesas
New Mexico: Acoma, Isleta, Laguna, Picuris, San Felipe, San Ildefonso, San Juan, Santo Domingo, Taos, Zuni (near Gallup)

Hispanic Towns
Throughout northern New Mexico and in the areas of cities in the Southwest, there are Hispanic villages and neighborhoods. Many retain the traditional architectural expressions. Listed here are only a few favorites.
Arizona: Tucson Barrio District
New Mexico: Albuquerque Old Town, Costilla Plaza, Las Cruces Old Town, Las Vegas Old Town, Mora Valley, Ranchos de Taos, Villanueva

Forts
Many Territorial forts have fallen into ruins, but some are preserved as State or National Monuments. Here are a selected few.
Arizona: Fort Lowell, Tucson; Tubac Presidio, Tubac
California: Fort Tejon, Lebec
Colorado: Fort Garland
New Mexico: Fort Stanton, near Las Cruces
Fort Union, near Springer
Texas: Fort Brown, Brownsville
Fort Davis National Historic Site
Utah: Fort Deseret, Deseret; Fort Douglas, Salt Lake City

Cities and Towns
We recommend that you drive or walk around these towns, and explore the streets and buildings.
Arizona: Bisbee, Jerome, Tubac, Tucson
California: Monterey Old Town Historic District, Sonora, San Juan Bautista Plaza Historic District
Colorado: San Luis, Trinidad
New Mexico: Las Vegas, Santa Fe, Socorro, Taos (see other listings)
Texas: San Antonio

Churches and Missions
Important examples of traditional architecture are often best preserved in these churches. A short selection follows.
Arizona: San Xavier del Bac, Tucson
Tumacacori Mission, Tubac
California: San Carlos Borromeo Mission, Carmel
La Purísima Concepción Mission, near Lampoc
San Diego Mission, San Gabriel Mission, Santa Bárbara Mission
New Mexico: Arroyo Hondo Church, Taos; Cristo Rey Church, Santa Fe; Guadalupe Church, Santa Fe; Ranchos de Taos Church; San Miguel Church, Santa Fe; Santa Cruz Church, Santa Cruz; Santuario de Chimayo, Chimayo
Texas: The Alamo, San Antonio; Mission Concepción, San Antonio; San Jose Mission National Historic Site, San Antonio

Houses
We recommend that you check with the National Register of Historic Places (at your library) for other ideas as well as those places we include here.
Arizona: Casa Cordova, Tucson; De Grazia Arts and Cultural Foundation, Tucson; Fremont House, Tucson; Hubbel Trading Post National Historic Site, Ganado; The Old Adobe Patio (C. O. Brown House), Tucson
California: Los Cerritos Ranch House, Long Beach; Lopez Adobe, San Fernando; Martinez Adobe; Petaluma Adobe; Rancho El Encino; Ygnacio Palomares Adobe, Pomona.
New Mexico: Damacio Vigil House, Santa Fe; Fechin Home, Taos; Kit Carson Foundation, including Martinez Hacienda, Blumenschein House, Kit Carson Home, Morada de Don Fernando; Las Palomas Educational Retreat Center, Taos; Park Service Headquarters, Santa Fe; Rancho de las Golondrinas, south of Santa Fe; University of New Mexico, Albuquerque
Texas: Magoffin Homestead, El Paso

Collections
Excellent collections of Southwestern arts and artifacts can be seen at the following institutions, among others.
Arizona: Amerind Foundation, Dragoon;
Heard Museum, Phoenix
Colorado: Denver Art Museum;
Taylor Art Center, Colorado Springs
New Mexico: Harwood Foundation, Taos; Millicent Rogers Museum, Taos; Museum of New Mexico, Santa Fe, including Museum of Fine Arts, Museum of Indian Arts and Culture, Museum of International Folk Art, Palace of the Governors; Wheelwright Museum, Santa Fe

Commercial Establishments
Many commercial enterprises in the Southwest are located in historic and interesting adobe buildings. Please explore!

Wherever you are in the Southwest, explore for yourself and discover! Wonderful surprises await your visit.

Bibliography

Adams, Robert Hickman, *Colorado Adobes: The Art and Architecture of Early Hispanic Colorado,* Boulder, Colorado University Press, 1974.

Ahlborn, Richard E., *Saints of San Xavier,* Tucson, Arizona, Southwest Museum Research Center, 1974.

Baer, Morley, with A. Fink and A. Elkington, *Adobes in the Sun,* San Francisco, Chronicle Books, 1972.

Bunting, Bainbridge, *Early Architecture in New Mexico,* Albuquerque, University of New Mexico Press, 1976.

—*John Gaw Meem: Southwestern Architect,* Albuquerque, University of New Mexico Press, School of American Research, 1983.

—*Of Earth and Timbers Made: New Mexico Architecture,* Albuquerque, University of New Mexico Press, 1974.

—*Taos Adobes: Spanish Colonial and Territorial Architecture of the Taos Valley,* Santa Fe, Museum of New Mexico Press, 1964.

Cobos, Rubén, *A Dictionary of New Mexico and Southern Colorado Spanish,* Santa Fe, Museum of New Mexico Press, 1983.

deBuys, William, *Enchantment and Exploitation: The Life and Hard Times of a New Mexico Mountain Range,* Albuquerque, University of New Mexico Press, 1985.

Dethier, Jean, *Down to Earth: Adobe Architecture,* trans. by Ruth Eaton, Centre Georges Pompidou, Paris, New York, Facts on File, 1983.

Eldridge, Charles C., and J. Schimmel with W. Truettner, *Art in New Mexico 1900–1945: Paths to Taos and Santa Fe,* Washington, D.C., National Museum of American Art, Smithsonian Institution, 1986.

Goodrich, Lloyd, and Doris Bry, *Georgia O'Keeffe,* New York, Whitney Museum of American Art Catalogue, 1970.

Gordon, W. Ellis, *Adobe Architecture: Its Design and Construction,* Washington, United States Department of Agriculture Bulletin, 1941.

Gray, Virginia, Alan Macrae and Wayne McCall, *Mud, Space and Spirit; Handmade Adobes,* Santa Barbara, California, Capra Press, 1976.

Griffen, Helen Smith, *Casas and Courtyards: Historic Adobe Houses of California,* Oakland, California, Biobooks, 1955.

Hall, Elizabeth Boyd, *Popular Arts of Spanish New Mexico,* Santa Fe, Museum of New Mexico Press, 1974.

Hopson, Rex C., *Adobe: A Comprehensive Bibliography,* Santa Fe, Lightning Tree Press, 1979.

Iowa, Jerome, *Ageless Adobe: History and Preservation in Southwestern Architecture,* Santa Fe, Sunstone Press, 1985.

Kino, Eusebio Francisco *Historical Memoir of Primería Alta,* trans. by Herbert E. Bolton, Berkeley, University of California Press, 1948 (reprint of the 1919 edition)

Kubler, George, *The Religious Architecture of New Mexico,* Albuquerque, University of New Mexico Press, School of American Research, 1972.

—*Mexican Architecture of the Sixteenth Century,* New Haven, Yale University Press, 1948.

Lumpkins, William T., *Modern Spanish-Pueblo Homes,* Santa Fe, Santa Fe Publishing Co., 1946.

—*Casa Del Sol: Your Guide to Passive Solar House Designs,* Santa Fe, Santa Fe Publishing Co., 1981.

McHenry, P. G., *Adobe: Build it Yourself,* Tucson, University of Arizona Press, 1973.

McNary, John C., *John Gaw Meem: His Style Development and Residential Architecture Between 1924 and 1940,* Albuquerque, University of New Mexico, (unpublished thesis), 1977.

Mather, Christine, and Sharon Woods, *Santa Fe Style,* New York, Rizzoli, 1986.

Meem, John Gaw, *Adobe Past and Present,* Santa Fe, Museum of New Mexico Press, 1972.

O'Conner, John F., *The Adobe Book,* Santa Fe, Ancient City Press, 1973.

O'Keeffe, Georgia, *Georgia O'Keeffe,* New York, Viking Press, 1976.

Ortiz, Alfonso, *The Tewa World: Space, Time, Being and Becoming in a Pueblo Society,* Chicago, University of Chicago Press, 1969.

—*New Perspectives on the Pueblos,* Albuquerque, University of New Mexico Press, 1972.

Rudofsky, Bernard, *Architecture Without Architects: An Introduction to Non-Pedigreed Architecture,* New York, Museum of Modern Art, 1964.

—*The Prodigious Builders,* New York, Harcourt Brace Jovanovich, 1977.

Sagel, Jim, *Tunomás Honey,* Binghamton, New York, Bilingual Press, 1983.

Sanders, Gordon, *Oscar Berninghaus: Master Painter of American Indians and the Frontier West,* Taos, Taos Heritage Publishing Co., 1985.

Sanford, Trent Elwood, *The Architecture of the Southwest: Indian, Spanish, American,* New York, W. W. Norton, 1950.

Shipway, Verna Cook, and Warren Shipway, *Decorative Designs in Mexican Homes,* New York, Architectural Book Publishing Company, 1978.

—*Houses of Mexico: Origins and Traditions,* New York, Architectural Book Publishing Company, 1982.

—*Mexican Homes of Today,* New York, Architectural Book Publishing Company, 1978.

—*Mexican Houses, Old and New,* New York, Architectural Book Publishing Company, 1982.

—*Mexican Interiors,* New York, Architectural Book Publishing Company, 1978.

Smith, Ed W., *Adobe Bricks in New Mexico,* Socorro, New Mexico Bureau of Mines and Minerals, 1982.

Spicer, Edward H., *Cycles of Conquest: The Impact of Spain, Mexico and the U. S. on the Indians of the Southwest, 1533–1960,* Tucson, University of Arizona Press, 1962.

Spicer, Ros, and Teresa Turner, *The People of Fort Lowell,* Tucson, Fort Lowell Historic District Board, 1974.

Steadman, Myrtle, *Adobe Architecture,* Santa Fe, Sunstone Press, 1973.

—*Adobe Fireplaces,* Santa Fe, Sunstone Press, 1974.

—*Adobe Remodeling,* Santa Fe, Sunstone Press, 1976.

Sturtevant, William C., and Alfonso Ortiz, *Handbook of North American Indians,* volumes 9 and 10, Washington, D. C., Smithsonian Institution, 1979–1984.

Vedder, Alan C., *Furniture of Spanish New Mexico,* Santa Fe, Sunstone Press, 1977.

Warren, Nancy Hunter, *New Mexico Style,* Santa Fe, Museum of New Mexico Press, 1986.

Index